UNSTUCK!

Unstuck!: Turning God-Given Dreams into Reality
Copyright © 2025 Bob Pittman Ministries

All rights reserved.

No part of this publication may be reproduced in a retrieval system, or transmitted in any form or by any means—electronic, mechanical, photocopying, recording, or otherwise—without the prior written permission of the publisher.

Scriptures taken from the Holy Bible, New International Version®, NIV®. Copyright © 1973, 1978, 1984, 2011 by Biblica, Inc.™ Used by permission of Zondervan. All rights reserved worldwide. www.zondervan.com The "NIV" and "New International Version" are trademarks registered in the United States Patent and Trademark Office by Biblica, Inc.™ | Scripture taken from the New King James Version®. Copyright © 1982 by Thomas Nelson. Used by permission. All rights reserved. | Scripture quotations from The Authorized (King James) Version. Rights in the Authorized Version in the United Kingdom are vested in the Crown. Reproduced by permission of the Crown's patentee, Cambridge University Press.

While precaution has been taken in the preparation of this book, the publisher and author assume no responsibility for errors or omissions, or for damages resulting from the use of the information contained herein.

This book is set in the typeface *Athelas* designed by Veronika Burian and Jose Scaglione.

Paperback ISBN: 978-1-967262-14-4

A Publication of *Tall Pine Books*
PO Box 42 Warsaw | Indiana 46581
www.tallpinebooks.com

| 1 25 25 20 16 02 |

Published in the United States of America

UNSTUCK!
Turning God-Given Dreams into Reality

BOB PITTMAN

ENDORSEMENTS

It is a joy for me to give you a good report on Bob Pittman's awesome new book. Your life will be encouraged by the insights within this book.

—Bobby Conner,
Eagles View Ministries

This manuscript by Pastor Bob Pittman is strategic guidance/plans to empower/navigate life's journey. Any of these chapters could be a book in itself; however, I really suggest all of them are an alignment for your destiny. Had I never known Bob, I would strongly recommend this book, but because I do know him and have seen evidence of this working in his life for many years… please read it thoroughly and get another one to give to a friend.

—Mickey Robinson,
Prophetic Destiny International

This is what it will say: *Unstuck* is an easy read that pushes hard against a culture of ambivalence and lethargy. I've known Bob Pittman for years, and this book is more than encouraging – it is an honest and faith-filled testimonial of what God can do when one trusts Him with our dreams. Bob admonishes the reader to dream righteously and to press into Him until the dream is fulfilled. *Unstuck* is a guide around traps and snares that keep so many stuck and a path forward. *Unstuck* makes that which previously seemed impossible, possible. I wholeheartedly recommend this life-changing read. No one should stay stuck!

—Pastor Philip Thompson

UNSTUCK is a practical manual to get unstuck! Dreams and visions could be realized by following clearly defined steps outlined in this book. I have observed the life of the author on a mission trip in East Africa. UNSTUCK epitomizes the life of Pastor Bob Pittman. All the bases covered in this book pay tribute to how he has moved forward in his life, ministry, and with his family. His success story can be yours too.

—Ron Kinnear
Founder of Africa Missions

It has been my privilege to enjoy a close friendship with Bob for over 25 years. Bob is a man with a passion to strengthen the church and to reach the lost, in his church at home or in some of the poorest nations around the world. Whether you are looking to start a ministry, a business, or just need to be encouraged in walking out your life with God, *Unstuck* will give you the tools and encouragement you need! It will help you to overcome obstacles and realize your God-given ability to succeed in whatever God is calling you to do.

—Jeff Oleson,
Businessman and President of TUF Ministry

My dear friend Bob, who has personally encouraged me often in my own moments of disappointment and struggles, has written an inspirational masterpiece! When reading through his manuscript, I kept thinking of a phrase I once heard: "Dream big, or you'll limit God." And indeed, Bob's book will help you dream big—and even bigger, and bigger!

This book is filled with Scripture, wisdom, strategies, and many practical stories and examples. One of my favorite lines in the book is where he writes, "Setbacks do not define me. They refine me. Every struggle holds the potential to shape something greater within you. Your dream is worth the fight."

So read this book cover to cover, and then prayerfully read it again... and go out and change the world! Oh—just one more thing—never quit!

—CARL WESLEY ANDERSON,
Founder of Born to Blaze Ministries, author of *Love Speaks: 21 Ways to Recognize God's Multi-Faceted Voice*, and filmmaker of the documentary film series of the same title, airing on some of the world's largest Christian networks.

CONTENTS

Endorsements v
Foreword 1
Introduction 7

Chapter 1: Stuck 13
Chapter 2: God Has a Dream and Purpose for Your Life 33
Chapter 3: The Power of Vision: See It Before You Build It!........ 49
Chapter 4: Faith: Move Mountains 69
Chapter 5: Believing in Yourself – Keys to Confidence 87
Chapter 6: The Courage To Do "The Hard Thing" 105
Chapter 7: Mentors – The Great Shortcut 115
Chapter 8: Breaking Bad Habits – Creating Good Habits............127
Chapter 9: Killing Procrastination 141
Chapter 10: Freedom from Limiting Beliefs........................ 151
Chapter 11: Plan and Conquer.....................................163
Chapter 12: One Small Step for Man,
One Large Step Toward Dream Fulfillment..........................175
Chapter 13: Time Management, Taming the Wild Stallion 185
Chapter 14: Taking Risks – Walking on Water..................... 199
Chapter 15: True Success 213
Chapter 16: Knowing God! 227

Tools For Success 237
Vision to Reality: A Dream Planning Worksheet 241
Time Management Daily Planner........................... 245

FOREWORD

by Michael L. Mathews,
Author of *And God Chose Dreams* and
VP of Technology and Innovation, *Oral Roberts University*

There are rare moments in life when a book doesn't just speak—it awakens. *Unstuck! Turning God-Given Dreams into Reality* is such a book.

From the moment I opened the manuscript and began reading Bob Pittman's deeply personal yet universally relatable journey, I sensed something sacred, holy, and personal unfolding. In these pages, Bob doesn't merely teach—he imparts, while inspiring anyone who may feel stuck. He doesn't just inspire; he ignites the very flame within each and every person. And most of all, he doesn't just share a message—he offers a divine roadmap that aligns perfectly with the heartbeat of God's calling for this generation.

My life has been dedicated to the convergence of innovation, faith, and purpose. As someone who has walked the corridors of technology, higher education, and global ministry—and been blessed to see dreams manifest from local churches to the halls of the United Nations—I have discovered one constant truth: when God gives a dream, it refuses to stay dormant. It may wait. It may wrestle. It may even get buried beneath life's hardened concrete.

But a God-given dream has resurrection power. Bob Pittman's book is a trumpet blast to remind every reader that this power is alive and available now.

Throughout *Unstuck!*, Bob's voice carries the compassion of a fatherly pastor, the precision of a businessman, and the fire of a prophet. He speaks as someone who has been in the trenches—not theorizing from a distance but testifying from personal trials and resurrection. His stories—from business setbacks to Burundi's mountaintops—are not tales of triumph for ego's sake, but evidence that God dreams in us, with us, and through us. And when we surrender to His dream, what once was stuck begins to flow again.

This message resonates deeply with me because I, too, know what it's like to carry a dream that seems too bold, too different, too delayed. When I wrote *And God Chose Dreams*, I was compelled by the divine insight that God doesn't randomly scatter ambitions—He seeds eternal purpose into the hearts of His people. We are not dreamers because of culture, ambition, or self-help mantras. We are dreamers because we are made in the image of a Creator who still dreams through us. We serve a Master Designer who wrote (stitched) a book about each of us while we were still in our mother's womb.

Bob's work is a masterful continuation of this truth. With every chapter, he chips away at the hardened places in our hearts—concrete poured by disappointment, fear, and false identity. He introduces wisdom not just as a concept, but as a weapon. He reminds us that mentorship matters, that faith is not fragile, and that procrastination is not a personality—it's a thief. In doing so, he offers the reader a practical toolkit for reclaiming forward motion.

What I especially appreciate about Bob's approach is how he integrates the seemingly "ordinary" roles of life—business, parenting, working retail or ministry—with the extraordinary invitation of destiny. He dismantles the myth that dreams only live in pulpits or palaces. Instead, he affirms what I've seen around the world: the kingdom of God moves through everyday people who dare to believe that God can do more than they ask or imagine.

To those reading this foreword, let me offer you a moment of pastoral clarity. If you've picked up this book and thought, "This is just another motivational message," I urge you to reconsider. What you hold in your hands is not just encouragement—it is divine strategy. Bob has married spirit and skill, testimony and tool, inspiration and instruction. And that combination? That's what gets people unstuck.

In every generation, God raises voices that echo His heart for freedom, purpose, and legacy. Bob Pittman is one of those voices for this moment. His words don't entertain—they equip. His stories don't just move us emotionally—they shift us spiritually. And most of all, his wisdom doesn't stop at the last page—it lingers in the reader's spirit, urging them to dream again, to try again, to rise again.

As someone who has spent my life helping individuals, universities, churches, and nations tap into the future God intended, I can testify to the power of vision partnered with faith. Bob doesn't just help you visualize your dream—he helps you build it with God. And in a world suffocating under the weight of discouragement and delay, that kind of guidance is priceless.

So, whether you're a burned-out leader, a discouraged entrepreneur, a restless pastor, or simply someone whose dream has grown quiet—this book is your invitation back to divine movement and destiny. This is your moment to believe again. And if you'll let it, *Unstuck!* will become more than a book—it will become a turning point with living words of momentum.

I find great interest in knowing this book was imagined and penned in the great State of Wisconsin. Wisconsin is home to many things related to spiritual awakening and innovation. Below are key history makers in the state of Wisconsin:

1. In 1898, Gideon's Bible ministry started in Boscobel, Wisconsin.[1]
2. In 1898, Pentecostal renewal started in the small town of Dallas, Wisconsin, where 30 people went into the ministry.[2] The Dallas Church started two years later in 1900.
3. Between 1840 and 1920, Wisconsin was the leading U.S. state to welcome Jewish immigrants. A total of 74 small communities welcomed Jewish immigrants.[3] The most famous Jewish immigrant was Golda Meir, who became Israel's Prime Minister from 1969–1974.[4]
4. On September 28, 1925, Seymour Cray, the father of the supercomputer and founder of Control Data and Cray Supercomputers, was born and changed every industry.[5]
5. In 1954, Steve Jobs, founder of Apple Computer, was born and spent the first seven years of his life in Wisconsin before moving to California.[6] Note: Steve Jobs was conceived

---

1. Boscobel, Beaver Dam and Beginning The Gideons International | Wisconsin Historical Society
2. Assemblies of God Heritage Magazine, Vol. 5, No. 3, Fal 1985
3. Jews in Wisconsin | Wisconsin Historical Society
4. Golda Meir | Wisconsin Historical Society
5. Seymour Cray | Biography, Invention, Supercomputers, & Facts | Britannica
6. 'On any little county or country road, there is so much history': Wisconsinite discovers Apple founder's true local connection | Washington Co. News | gmtoday.com

in Wisconsin, delivered at birth in California, then brought back and adopted.
6. In 2025, Pastor Pittman pens the book *Unstuck* that motivates all Wisconsinites to step into their God-given dreams.

Thank you, Bob, for not giving up on your own dream so that others might remember theirs.

To every reader, remember this: You are not too late. You are not too broken. And you are not disqualified. God has a dream buried inside of you—and with faith, wisdom, and the courage to take the next step, you will see it come alive.

Keep dreaming—and never stop moving.

With honor and expectancy,
Michael L. Mathews
Author of *And God Chose Dreams*
Vice President for Global Learning and Innovation

INTRODUCTION

"All your dreams can come true if you have the courage to pursue them."

— Walt Disney

Everyone has a dream. Some dreams are bold, daring pursuits: building a business, launching a ministry, running a marathon, achieving financial freedom, or exploring the world. Others are quieter but just as profound—breaking free from doubt, discovering purpose, writing a book, or stepping into a calling long left unspoken. For many, dreams remain just that—dreams. Unfulfilled. Unpursued. Stuck.

Throughout my journeys, whether on business or ministry trips, or in everyday conversations, I've met people from all walks of life who struggle. Not because they lack talent or passion, but because no one has ever believed in or mentored them. Some were told their dreams were too big. Others were made to feel small. But here's the truth: Your dream matters. You matter. You were created for something greater. Within you are the gifts God has given you to pursue and fulfill your dream or calling. With encouragement and the right training, you can make it happen. Now is the time to take your life to the next level.

Encouragement sticks to the ribs:

When I was 17, I spent the day with my uncle Sonny in Bloomington, Minnesota. He was a remarkable man—uniquely brilliant, a design engineer with numerous patents in diesel automotive technology. He was meticulous, always able to fix anything. In the 1970s, he was part of a team that set the land speed world record in the 4-cylinder diesel class. He seemed capable of anything.

An ex-military man, a race car builder, a man of unwavering integrity—we all deeply respected him. That day, as I helped him work on a race car, we talked about nothing in particular, just small talk. Then, suddenly, he leaned in and studied me for a moment. "Bob," he said, "you're not like the others. You are unique. You have giftings, and I believe you can go far if you apply yourself." Just as quickly, he shifted the conversation back to jokes, and we continued working until it was time for me to leave.

But those words stayed with me—burning in my heart that night and for years to come. I'm sure he told my siblings and half the neighborhood something similar, ha! But for me, hearing it from him was different. His words ignited a spark of confidence in a shy, insecure young man.

Years later, when I graduated from college, his words echoed in my mind. They had become more than encouragement; they were a prophecy that had shaped my journey. It was the encouragement I needed to chase my dreams and a desire to inspire others.

Why Did I Write This Book?

Mentoring has always been at the core of our hearts. My wife and I find deep fulfillment in helping others step into their God-given dreams and purpose. Throughout our journey, we've built small businesses, navigated the corporate world in technology—where I served in various capacities of management, later became VP of Sales & Marketing, and business partner in a software company—and dedicated ourselves to ministry. Between the two of us, we've worn many hats: youth leaders, associate pastor, Bible college teacher, senior pastor, missionary, conference speaker, and yes—even church bathroom cleaner.

We also raised two incredible sons, whom I am very proud of. Ministry has taken us to about 15 nations, each one leaving a lasting imprint on my heart. People often ask me which country is my favorite, and I always say, "All of them—because people live there." But if I could take you on one unforgettable journey, it would be deep into the mountains of Burundi, Africa, where we've worked among the remote pygmy tribes. My oldest son joined me on my first trip there, an experience that undoubtedly shaped his life. They gave him opportunities to speak, and later—much to his surprise—gave him the chance to ride the back of a massive crocodile!

And then there's my wife—my remarkable Cajun warrior. She grew up in poverty, in a home shadowed by hardship. Her father was an angry alcoholic and a gambler until, by God's grace, he found redemption later in life. I have witnessed firsthand how grace transforms, and my wife is living proof. I'll never forget the day our spiritual father, Bobby Conner, spoke over her: "You have thick skin and a soft heart."

She is relentless in her work ethic, courageous in spirit, a great mother, and—if you ask me—the best Cajun cook in America (just my opinion, but I stand by it!). Most of her younger adult life has been spent running small businesses and serving in the church, each a testament to her grit and determination and love.

One of my favorite moments happened in Argentina, at a large church we were visiting. Without warning, the pastor invited—well, instructed—her to share her testimony. Fear threatened to overwhelm her, but she faced it head-on. As she spoke, tears filled the sanctuary, and hearts were transformed. It was one of the most powerful meetings I've ever witnessed.

This book is born out of these moments, our journey, and a desire to empower others. If our stories, struggles, and victories can inspire even one person to step boldly into their calling and fulfill their dreams, then every page will have been worth writing.

The Challenge of Moving Forward:

Many people get stuck in fear, failure, or fatigue. They hesitate because stepping into the unknown feels risky. They doubt their ability because the voices of discouragement have been louder than the whispers of faith. And yet, some of the greatest Christian entrepreneurs and athletes faced similar obstacles—but refused to settle.

Take David Green, the founder of Hobby Lobby. He started with nothing, building his business on biblical principles. Despite financial struggles early on, he persevered, tithing faithfully and trusting that obedience would lead to success. Today, Hobby Lobby is a multi-billion-dollar company, and Green has dedicated his life to generosity and kingdom impact. His story is a testament that a dream, rooted in faith and persistence, can transform lives.

Or consider Kurt Warner, the Super Bowl-winning quarterback who once worked stocking shelves in a grocery store. Before his NFL career took off, he faced rejection after rejection. His story could have ended in frustration, but Warner kept believing—even when his circumstances looked impossible. His persistence paid off, and today, he not only holds championship titles but also impacts countless lives through his faith-based outreach.

Faith, Action, and the Journey Ahead:

This book isn't just about fulfilling dreams—it's about how to live out God's best for your life. "Unstuck! Turning God-Given Dreams into Reality" is about stepping past fear, breaking through limitations, and embracing the life God intended for you. Whether you're starting a business, changing careers, or simply searching for purpose, this journey requires faith, action, and resilience.

I've seen firsthand what happens when people refuse to settle. I've met leaders whose vision shaped industries, missionaries who changed nations, and entrepreneurs who built businesses on faith. Their stories prove one thing—when you trust God and step forward, your dream is no longer just a possibility—it's a promise, a reality.

So, let's take this journey together. Let's uncover what's holding you back, confront your doubts, and step into the future with courage. Because your life is meant for more—and now is the time to embrace the next level.

CHAPTER 1

STUCK

"Many of life's failures are people who did not realize how close they were to success when they gave up." —Thomas Edison

There's nothing quite like the feeling of being stuck. It's frustrating, demoralizing, and often suffocating—like being trapped in mud that refuses to let go, or worse, cement that hardens around you. You see the world moving forward, but you're paralyzed, unable to make progress.

Everyone faces moments like this. Some experience setbacks in business, others struggle in personal growth, and many wrestle with faith, wondering if God has forgotten them. But being stuck is not the end. It's a moment, not a destination.

The Weight of Disappointment:

Disappointment is one of the biggest causes of feeling stuck. Michael Jordan, widely regarded as the greatest basketball player of all time, was cut from his high school basketball team—a devastating blow. For many, that kind of rejection could be enough to quit. To give up on their dream. But instead of accepting defeat, he used the pain as fuel. He trained harder, focused sharper, and later led his teams to six NBA championships.

On the business side, Dave Ramsey, a leading Christian financial expert, found himself bankrupt in his early career. His dream of financial success crumbled around him, and he faced the kind of failure that could have permanently wrecked his future. Again, he could have given up. Many would have. Instead of giving up, he pushed ahead, rebuilt, and learned from his failures. He began applying biblical financial principles and found freedom. Today, he is helping millions find financial freedom.

When Faith Feels Paralyzed:

Even spiritually, people get stuck. The weight of uncertainty, pain, and setbacks can make the promise of something greater seem impossibly distant. Joseph, the dreamer in Genesis, knew this feeling intimately. His vision of leadership—of a future where he would stand tall—was shattered the moment his own brothers betrayed him, selling him into slavery as if his existence meant nothing. The chains on his wrists weren't just physical; they were the embodiment of rejection, loss, and confusion. Years passed, and prison walls became his reality, a space where dreams felt like cruel illusions. Every day seemed to have a voice that said, "You will never fulfill your dreams. Give up, and get angry." But even in the silence of his suffering, Joseph refused to let discouragement consume him. He didn't allow bitterness to take root; instead, he held on to the quiet whisper that God's purpose was bigger than his circumstances.

Faith isn't about just seeing the outcome—it's about trusting in the unseen, and Joseph did exactly that. Through betrayal, imprisonment, and forgotten promises, he chose to believe that God had not abandoned him. Each passing year was a test, a call to persevere even when everything seemed lost. And then, one day, the dream awakened. Joseph's patience, endurance, and unwavering trust in God led him to a position of authority—one that would allow him to save nations from famine and change history. His story is a reminder that setbacks are not the end of the road; they are the moments that shape us, refine us, and prepare us for the fulfillment of a purpose greater than we could ever imagine. Like Joseph, we must press through.

Setbacks have a way of planting doubts in our minds. They whisper questions we never asked before: *What if I'm not good enough? What if I fail again? What if this dream was never meant for me?* Left unchecked, these thoughts multiply, shaping a narrative of discouragement. Over time, discouragement hardens into hopelessness, and suddenly, we find ourselves trapped—not in a physical prison, but in an invisible cage of emotion, unable to move forward.

This is where the battle begins. Because hopelessness is a thief—it steals ambition, stifles creativity, and convinces us that settling is safer than trying. But this is not where your story ends. **You cannot allow this.** Your dreams, your passions, and your purpose are too valuable to let slip away.

When setbacks strike, remind yourself: *They do not define me. They refine me.* Every struggle holds the potential to shape something greater within you. Your dream is worth the fight. Your life is worth the effort. And no temporary obstacle should have the power to rewrite the destiny meant for you.

Pastor Joel Osteen once shared how his father, John Osteen, dreamed of building a ministry. For years, no doors opened. He preached to empty seats and faced financial hardship. But he refused to quit on the vision God placed in his heart. He learned how to stand in faith and trust God. He learned how to push through obstacles. He didn't quit. Later in his life, he fulfilled all that God placed in his heart. Today, the ministry is still impacting millions around the world.

Getting Unstuck: A Personal Experience

In my own life, I've faced moments when my dream felt out of reach—where progress seemed impossible. During my time in the software industry, we poured our hearts into launching the company. At first, things went well, and success seemed within grasp. But then, outside circumstances shifted, and suddenly, our momentum stalled. The business went flat.

The excitement that once fueled us began to fade, replaced by the weight of obligations—payroll, overhead, bills upon bills. We felt stuck, knowing something had to change.

I prayed, fasted, and believed God would give us direction. It was a difficult season. I wrestled with the idea of quitting and working a regular, stable job. Deep inside, I knew somehow God would do something. Then, finally, wisdom came. My business partner and I were on a plane discussing possible solutions. After a long conversation, we did something simple but transformative—we took out a napkin and wrote down a new plan and strategy for the company. It felt right. I knew this was a gift from the Lord.

The changes were hard. They required sacrifice, tough decisions, and a strong focus on one main goal. The benefits didn't come quickly—not in a few weeks, not in a month. It was a grueling process. But after six months, we saw daylight, and after a year, we started achieving our business goals. The company grew strong and healthy until the day I resigned to go into full-time ministry.

That experience showed me that being stuck is never permanent; there is always a way forward. When uncertainty clouds the path ahead, wisdom is the key to breaking through. James 1:5 reminds us: *"If any of you lack wisdom, let him ask of God, that giveth to all men liberally, and upbraideth not; and it shall be given him."*

God doesn't leave us without direction. His plan leads to fruitfulness and fulfillment, and sometimes, all it takes is one word—one piece of wisdom—to shift everything. For us, the answer wasn't winning the lottery or stumbling upon hidden treasure. It was a new strategy, the right approach at the right time.

No matter the situation, the right idea or the right wisdom will pull you out of feeling stuck and open the door to the next step forward.

Concrete Won't Hold You Forever:

If getting stuck in the mud is frustrating, getting stuck in concrete is terrifying. It feels permanent, hopeless, and like time has run out. But here's the truth: God specializes in breaking hardened places.

In the early years of their ministry, Brian and Bobbie Houston faced obstacles that would have been enough to discourage anyone. Financial setbacks loomed large, and the weight of uncertainty pressed down on them daily. The vision they carried for Hillsong Church was bold, but the reality they lived in was filled with challenges—empty bank accounts, unanswered questions, and moments of doubt that threatened to slow their progress. Growing a church wasn't just about a Sunday gathering; it was about faith in action, trusting that God was building something greater even when things looked bleak.

There were nights of prayer, where they wrestled with God for direction, and days of hard work, where every step forward seemed met with resistance. But despite the struggles, they refused to let discouragement define their mission. Hillsong wasn't built overnight—it was shaped through years of faith, resilience, and the belief that worship could transform lives. Slowly, through the power of music, resources, and dynamic preaching, their ministry expanded beyond what they could have imagined. Today, millions have been touched by Hillsong's worship, its messages, and the unwavering example of faith through trials. Their journey serves as a testament to God's ability to turn obstacles into opportunities, proving that even when you're stuck, trust and perseverance can lead to something extraordinary.

Colonel Sanders' story is one of perseverance against all odds. At 65 years old, most people would have settled into retirement, but he refused to believe that his best days were behind him. With nothing more than a dream and a fried chicken recipe, he traveled across the country, knocking on doors, presenting his idea, and hearing rejection—over and over again. More than 1,000 times, he was told "no," that his recipe wouldn't work, that his vision was unrealistic. Any reasonable person might have given up after the first hundred failures, but Sanders pressed on, driven by an unwavering belief that his idea mattered.

And then, finally, someone said "yes." That single opportunity turned into what we now recognize as one of the most successful fast-food chains in history. But his legacy wasn't just about chicken—it was about endurance, about having faith when the world tells you to quit. Later in life, Sanders used his wealth to support mission projects, ensuring that his success wasn't just personal but a means to bless others. His journey is a testament that failure isn't final, and sometimes, the breakthrough comes only after we've been tested beyond what seems possible.

Don't look at setbacks as concrete. There is always a better way to do things, a better product to invent, or a new twist in ministry that draws the masses.

Being stuck doesn't mean you've failed—it simply means it's time for a new approach. This truth is so important, yet many struggle to embrace it.

From Stuck to Thriving: The Story of Pastor Jim Cymbala and The Brooklyn Tabernacle:

In the early 1970s, Jim Cymbala stepped into a struggling church in Brooklyn, New York. At the time, The Brooklyn Tabernacle was small, financially unstable, and barely surviving, with fewer than 30 members. Many would have viewed it as a lost cause, but Cymbala saw something deeper—an opportunity for God to provide wisdom and change an impossible situation.

Overwhelmed by the challenges, Cymbala felt led to build the church on prayer rather than strategy alone. Instead of focusing solely on traditional growth tactics, he encouraged his small congregation to seek God fervently, believing that prayer changes everything. Midweek prayer meetings became the heart of the ministry, drawing people from all walks of life. Through this shift, something extraordinary happened—the church began to experience revival. The congregation grew, not through marketing or programs, but through genuine spiritual transformation. People wanted to encounter the living God. People struggling with addiction, brokenness, and hopelessness found healing, purpose, and community.

Over the years, The Brooklyn Tabernacle expanded into a thriving, multi-ethnic church with thousands of members. It became known for authentic worship, passionate prayer, and life-changing outreach programs.

A key part of the church's impact came through music. Cymbala's wife, Carol Cymbala, faced her fears and began leading a choir, which grew into the renowned Brooklyn Tabernacle Choir. This choir, made up of everyday people rather than professional singers, became a global influence, winning six Grammy Awards and recording 40 albums that touched millions.

All of their success came as they began to seek God for a new approach. They didn't stay stuck in the concrete of disappointment, but pressed on, and God used their church to touch the world.

A New Approach:

I've sat with countless talented, intelligent, and ambitious entrepreneurs who were on the verge of giving up on their dreams. Some, with tears in their eyes, would say, "I just can't make this business work!" Yet, their struggle wasn't due to a lack of skill or determination—it was because they were using the wrong approach. They needed one thing: God's wisdom. One idea from God can change everything. One small change can mean the difference between failure and success.

One powerful example of rethinking strategy comes from the coffee shop industry. Traditionally, coffee shops focus on creating a welcoming seating area and serving great coffee. While that model still works, studies now show that adding a drive-thru window can increase sales by 50-70%. This simple shift transforms business by catering to convenience and speed, proving that success often requires adapting to new demands.

We can't afford to be locked into tradition or personal preferences—sometimes, breaking free from the familiar is the only way to move forward.

The First Step Out of "Stuck:"

No matter how long you've been trapped, rejected, disappointed, or lost, there is a way out. Fear and disappointment often lead to hesitation, doubt, and paralysis, preventing individuals from stepping into their God-given dreams. Second Timothy 1:7 says, "For God has not given us a spirit of fear, but of power and of love and of a sound mind." Isaiah 41:10 says, "Do not fear, for I am with you; do not be dismayed, for I am your God." Both scriptures are key to moving forward. You must regain your confidence and determine, "I will not quit!"

- "In leadership, you must have thick skin and a soft heart."—Bobby Conner
- "It always seems impossible until it's done."—Nelson Mandela
- "You just can't beat the person who won't give up."—Babe Ruth
- "Tough times never last, but tough people do."—Robert H. Schuller
- "You can never quit. Winners never quit, and quitters never win."— Ted Turner

- "Many of life's failures are people who did not realize how close they were to success when they gave up."—Thomas Edison
- "There's no magic to running far or climbing Everest. Endurance is mental strength. It's all about heart."—Bear Grylls
- "In any moment of decision, the best thing you can do is the right thing, the next best thing is the wrong thing, and the worst thing you can do is nothing." —Theodore Roosevelt
- "It is hard to fail, but it is worse never to have tried to succeed."— Theodore Roosevelt
- "Faith, combined with action, moves mountains." - Unknown

Divine Encouragement:

In 2012, while serving in full-time ministry, I found myself walking through some difficult challenges. At the time, a well-known minister, Bob Jones, was scheduled to speak at a conference hosted by my friends, Pastors Bidal and Sherry Torrez. I had met Bob years before, and I felt a strong desire to reconnect.

I reached out and arranged a meeting with him during the upcoming conference. It was an important moment for me. I wanted him to pray over me, to speak something fresh and encouraging into my life. I prayed earnestly, asking God to use this meeting as a source of strength.

The day finally arrived. In the quiet of the pastor's office, Bob Jones and I exchanged small talk. But then, without warning, he looked me straight in the eyes, cutting through all the niceties. He stepped into the middle of the room and commanded, "Push on my chest." He was in his eighties. I was in my mid-forties, strong and in good shape. I hesitated, gently pushing against him. "I said, push on my chest!" His tone was firmer. I pressed a little harder. Then, with sudden intensity, he barked, "I said, push!" So I did—I shoved him across the room and pinned him against the wall for what felt like a full minute. Then, just as abruptly, he broke into laughter.

"There it is," he said, grinning. "That's it. If you want a breakthrough, you've got to learn to mean business and push through."

His words settled deep in my spirit, and I knew it was the Lord speaking to me. That moment wasn't just an illustration—it was a life lesson, a challenge, and an answer to the prayer I had whispered before the meeting.

The difference between those who remain stuck and those who break free is not talent, luck, or special advantages—it's the fact that with faith, strategy, and persistence, anything is possible.

Getting Unstuck: The Right Mindset—Solomon

There are moments in history when a single shift in mindset changes everything. One of the most powerful examples of this is found in the reign of King Solomon. Before Solomon ascended the throne, Israel was stagnant, "stuck." Its economy was not flourishing, and its national influence was limited. But then, something extraordinary happened. Solomon asked God for wisdom, and in response, God granted him unparalleled understanding. This wisdom didn't just shape Solomon's personal life—it transformed an entire nation.

The Turning Point: Solomon's Request for Wisdom

When Solomon became king, he recognized that leadership required more than a powerful military; it demanded wisdom. In 1 Kings 3:9, Solomon prayed, "Give your servant a discerning heart to govern your people and to distinguish between right and wrong." God answered his request, and the results were astonishing.

With divine wisdom, Solomon implemented policies that strengthened Israel's economy, expanded its influence, and ushered in an era of prosperity. His ability to make sound decisions, negotiate trade agreements, and manage resources led to unprecedented growth. Israel became one of the wealthiest nations of its time.

The Power of a Wise Mindset

Solomon's story teaches us that the right mindset can change everything. Wisdom is more than knowledge—it is the ability to apply understanding in a way that leads to success. Whether in leadership, business, or personal growth, implementing godly wisdom brings clarity, direction, and prosperity.

The lesson is clear: When we feel "stuck," we must seek wisdom. Just as Solomon's mindset transformed Israel, adopting a mindset of discipline, strategy, and godly insight can lead to breakthroughs in our own lives. The question is—will we ask for wisdom and apply it?

Keys to Becoming Unstuck:

When setbacks leave us feeling trapped, the way forward requires intentional action. To break free, we need the right mindset, the right wisdom, and the willingness to leave failure behind. But just as important, we must embrace planning and persistence—because dreams don't happen by accident.

1. Adopt the Right Mindset

Becoming unstuck starts in the mind. If you believe that failure is permanent, it will be. But if you shift your perspective and view challenges as stepping stones rather than roadblocks, new possibilities emerge. Growth begins when you acknowledge that your past does not define your future.

2. Seek the Right Wisdom

Wisdom is the key to navigating challenges. Sometimes, it comes through personal reflection, a mentor, or a fresh strategy. Other times, it's divine insight—a word from God that unlocks a new direction. Proverbs 4:7 reminds us: "Wisdom is the principal thing; therefore get wisdom: and with all thy getting get understanding." The right wisdom at the right moment can change everything.

3. Leave Failure Behind

Set your heart to move forward. Failure is a moment, not a destination. Too often, people let past mistakes paralyze them, believing they'll never recover. But failure is only final if you stop moving forward. Instead of letting it weigh you down, take the lessons it offers and step forward with renewed purpose. Your dream is still alive—and it's waiting for you to chase it again.

4. Heal

Healing from failure is not about ignoring the pain or pretending it never happened. True healing begins when you acknowledge the wounds—the disappointments, the broken dreams, the weight of past mistakes. When failure grips the soul, it often chains you to fear, convincing you that trying again will only lead to more heartache. But pretending the wounds don't exist only makes them fester. You can't move forward while dragging the baggage of regret behind you.

Breaking free starts with confronting the emotions honestly. Let yourself feel the grief, the frustration, the loss—but don't let them define you. Surrender them to God, laying each wound before Him, trusting that He can bring beauty even from brokenness. Healing comes in layers, through forgiveness—of others, but also of yourself. The enemy wants you to believe that failure is final, that your past disqualifies you from God's purpose. But God specializes in redemption. He turns ashes into beauty, setbacks into stepping stones.

Freedom to try again isn't about eliminating risk—it's about walking forward in faith despite it. When you let God heal the places that feel beyond repair, confidence begins to replace fear. You realize that failure wasn't the end—it was a chapter. And now, with healing, you are ready to turn the page.

5. Plan Your Path Forward

Having a dream is powerful, but without a plan, it remains only a dream. Success requires strategy—knowing where you want to go and mapping out the steps to get there. Break your goal into small, manageable actions, and set deadlines to keep yourself accountable. A well-thought-out plan removes uncertainty and builds momentum, turning your vision into reality.

For business ventures, a strong business plan is essential. It serves as a roadmap, guiding decision-making and ensuring financial sustainability. A business plan outlines your mission, target market, revenue strategy, operational structure, and growth plan—helping you stay focused and adapt when challenges arise. It also strengthens your ability to secure funding, attract partners, and set achievable milestones.

Planning ahead doesn't just shape your goals—it keeps you moving forward with clarity and purpose. Whether for business or personal success, intentional planning transforms aspirations into tangible results.

6. Never Quit

The only guaranteed way to fail is to stop trying. Obstacles will come, setbacks will happen, but persistence separates those who succeed from those who give up. Galatians 6:9 encourages us: *"And let us not be weary in well doing: for in due season we shall reap, if we faint not."* Success isn't about avoiding hardship—it's about pushing through when things get tough. Stay the course, hold onto your vision, and refuse to quit.

Advice from every successful entrepreneur:

- Never quit. Never quit. Never quit. Never quit. Never quit. Never quit. Never quit.
- Never quit. Never quit. Never quit. Never quit. Never quit. Never quit. Never quit.

- Never quit. Never quit. Never quit. Never quit. Never quit. Never quit. Never quit.
- Never quit. Never quit. Never quit. Never quit. Never quit. Never quit. Never quit.
- Never quit. Never quit. Never quit. Never quit. Never quit. Never quit. Never quit.
- Never quit. Never quit. Never quit. Never quit. Never quit. Never quit. Never quit.
- Never quit. Never quit. Never quit. Never quit. Never quit. Never quit. Never quit.
- Never quit. Never quit. Never quit. Never quit. Never quit. Never quit. Never quit.
- Never quit. Never quit. Never quit. Never quit. Never quit. Never quit. Never quit.
- Never quit. Never quit. Never quit. Never quit. Never quit. Never quit. Never quit.
- Never quit. Never quit. Never quit. Never quit. Never quit. Never quit. Never quit.
- Never quit. Never quit. Never quit. Never quit. Never quit. Never quit. Never quit.
- Never quit. Never quit. Never quit. Never quit. Never quit. Never quit. Never quit.
- Never quit. Never quit. Never quit. Never quit. Never quit. Never quit. Never quit.
- Never quit. Never quit.

Small Group Discussion & Devotional: "Stuck"

"Many of life's failures are people who did not realize how close they were to success when they gave up."

—Thomas Edison

OPENING PRAYER:

Begin by inviting the Holy Spirit to guide the conversation and bring encouragement, clarity, and wisdom to each person.

1. Opening Question:

- Can you describe a time when you felt "stuck" in life—emotionally, spiritually, or professionally? What did it feel like? How did you escape?

2. Reflection on the Chapter:

- What story or example from this chapter resonated with you the most (Joseph, Michael Jordan, Dave Ramsey, Pastor Jim Cymbala, etc.)? Why?
- Which quote or scripture encouraged you the most?

3. Personal Insight:

- How do you typically respond when you hit a setback? (Give up, double down, isolate, seek God, etc.)

- What fears or thoughts have ever convinced you to stop pursuing a dream or goal?

4. Digging Deeper – Key Scriptures:

Read:

- James 1:5 – "If any of you lacks wisdom…"
- 2 Timothy 1:7 – "For God has not given us a spirit of fear…"
- Galatians 6:9 – "Let us not grow weary in well doing…"

Discussion Questions:

- Which of these scriptures speaks to your current season?
- What kind of wisdom or direction are you seeking right now?

5. Action & Encouragement:

- What's one practical step you can take this week to get "unstuck" in an area of your life?
- Who can you ask to walk with you or pray for you as you take that step?

CLOSING CHALLENGE:

"You are closer than you think. Don't let temporary obstacles keep you from fulfilling your dream. Push through. Wisdom is coming."

Prayer Time:

Take a few minutes to pray over each other. Ask God for clarity, strength, and divine strategy for each person's situation.

CHAPTER 2

GOD HAS A DREAM AND PURPOSE FOR YOUR LIFE

"For I know the plans I have for you," declares the Lord, *"plans to prosper you and not to harm you, plans to give you hope and a future."*

—JEREMIAH 29:11

There comes a moment in everyone's life when they ask, "Why am I here? What is my purpose?" Some people drift through life with no clear direction, while others spend years pursuing something, only to realize they were chasing the wrong dream. The good news is—God has a plan for your life, and it's bigger than you think.

In this chapter, we will discuss the importance of knowing God's purposes for your life. My dreams are always tied to His purposes for me. When I align the two, I can make great progress.

The Blueprint of Destiny:

God is not random. He is intentional and strategic. Jeremiah 29:11 declares:

"For I know the plans I have for you," declares the Lord, "plans to prosper you and not to harm you, plans to give you hope and a future." This isn't just a comforting verse—it's a blueprint for destiny. God designed you with purpose, and He didn't make a mistake when He created you. Your talents, passions, and even your struggles all play a role in shaping your calling.

There are at least three areas of purpose in our lives. The first is serving God. The second is to love and serve others, and the third is our specific calling.

1. Our Ultimate Purpose: Serving God

Before we seek success or fulfillment, our highest calling is to serve God. He created us not only for accomplishments but for relationship—to know Him, love Him, and glorify Him in all we do. When we get this right, our life begins to make sense. Serving God leads to peace, purpose, and prevents aimless wandering.

> Matthew 6:33 – "Seek first the kingdom of God and his righteousness, and all these things will be added to you."

> Colossians 3:23-24 – "Whatever you do, work heartily, as for the Lord and not for men . . . You are serving the Lord Christ."

> Psalm 37:4 – "Delight yourself in the Lord, and He will give you the desires of your heart."

2. Our Purpose is to Love and Serve Others

God's dream for us is never just about ourselves. He desires that we use our blessings, talents, and careers to uplift others. Whether through kindness, generosity, leadership, or mentoring, impacting people is central to God's plan.

Why Blessing Others Matters:

- We reflect God's love when we serve others.
- We experience true fulfillment when we make a difference in someone's life.
- Our giftings were never meant for selfish gain, but for building up others.

Quotes On Serving Others:

- No one has ever become poor by giving.—Anne Frank
- Life's most persistent and urgent question is, what are you doing for others?—Martin Luther King Jr.
- We make a living by what we get, but we make a life by what we give.—Winston Churchill
- Service to others is the rent you pay for your room here on earth. — Muhammad Ali
- Only a life lived for others is a life worthwhile.—Albert Einstein
- The greatest among you will be your servant.—Jesus Christ (Matthew 23:11)
- Happiness doesn't result from what we get, but from what we give. —Ben Carson

The Bible is very clear on this subject. It is God's will, His desire, His purpose for you to love and serve others.

- Genesis 12:2 – "I will bless you . . . so that you will be a blessing."
- Acts 20:35 – "It is more blessed to give than to receive."
- Proverbs 11:25 – "Whoever refreshes others will be refreshed."

3. A Unique Purpose and Calling: "Where Dreams are Born."

God has a unique calling on each individual. The Earth's population is over eight billion. Every human has a unique fingerprint. And every person has a unique calling. God, in His wisdom, hid talents in you that could impact the world. When we identify our calling, we find that we have the correct abilities that go with the calling.

Your career is not random—it is your mission field.

I knew I was called to be a pastor when I was very young. I went to Bible College and served in our church in many capacities. I was a youth leader, a young adult leader, and then an associate pastor, all on a voluntary basis. I was not employed by a church until I was 40. During that time, God opened many doors in business. I was in product management, marketing, and sales, and later, a partner in a software company. For years, I traveled the country on a private corporate jet. As a young man, this was pretty exciting. It was hard work and long hours, but I felt like I was right where God wanted me to be.

At times, I would feel that inner call to ministry and become frustrated and wonder why God hadn't opened the door to full-time ministry. Many of my friends from college were already serving in a church. I prayed about this on a regular basis. One day, the Lord spoke to my heart. He clearly showed me that I was walking in His purpose and calling for that season. I was in a type of full-time ministry. My life was ministry, and my job was my mission field. Our occupation is a part of His plan. Whether you work at a church or in business, if you are serving the Lord, you are in ministry.

As I worked in the secular arena, many business trips became mission trips. I ministered to many broken businesspeople and won several to Christ on planes, at airports, even during sales calls. When you align calling and career, you feel joy, passion, and purpose.

> Ephesians 2:10 – "For we are His workmanship, created in Christ Jesus for good works, which God prepared beforehand."
>
> Jeremiah 29:11 – "For I know the plans I have for you, declares the Lord ... plans for welfare and not for evil, to give you a future and a hope."
>
> Romans 12:6 – "Having gifts that differ according to the grace given to us, let us use them."

Example: Esther

Esther was placed in the palace for a divine reason—to save her people. Her career (as queen) was perfectly matched with her calling. She stepped into purpose when she realized God had positioned her "for such a time as this" (Esther 4:14).

Examples of those who found their unique calling:

Billy Graham:

Billy Graham's story is a powerful reminder that God's plans often unfold in ways we could never predict. As a young boy growing up on a dairy farm in North Carolina, Graham lived a simple life, far removed from the grand stages he would later stand upon. His early years were ordinary—filled with hard work, family, and a future that, at the time, seemed destined to remain in small-town simplicity. But God saw something greater. A single moment, an encounter with faith, set him on a path toward something far beyond his own understanding.

At first, Graham had no idea where that path would lead. He was just a teenager attending revival meetings when he felt the pull of God's calling. That stirring grew into a deep conviction, leading him to study theology and prepare for ministry. But even then, he couldn't have imagined preaching to millions, advising presidents, and shaping generations of faith. His journey was one of obedience—taking one step at a time, trusting that each door God opened was leading him toward his true purpose. The road wasn't always clear, but Graham's unwavering trust allowed him to walk forward with confidence, knowing that God's dream for his life was unfolding with each decision to serve.

In the end, Billy Graham didn't just fulfill a dream; he stepped into a divine calling. His life proves that God's purpose isn't reserved for the extraordinary—it finds those who are willing to listen, obey, and trust the journey, even when the destination is unclear. The same principle applies to every life: The dream God has for us may be bigger than we imagine, but it begins with simple obedience.

Truet Cathy and Chick-fil-A:

Truett Cathy's story is a testament to the power of faith-driven entrepreneurship. He didn't have the advantage of wealth, power, or prestige when he started his journey. In fact, his beginnings were humble—a small restaurant, a simple menu, and a relentless commitment to serving others with excellence. What set him apart wasn't just his business ability, but his unwavering dedication to biblical principles. Integrity, generosity, and honoring God weren't just personal values; they became the foundation upon which Chick-fil-A was built.

Despite the challenges of growing a business in a competitive industry, Cathy never compromised his faith. His decision to keep Chick-fil-A closed on Sundays was more than just a policy—it was a bold statement that his priorities were rooted in honoring God. Over the years, his faithfulness bore fruit, turning his small restaurant into a billion-dollar enterprise. But true success wasn't measured by profit alone. Through Chick-fil-A, Cathy created opportunities to give back, support missions, and invest in communities. His business became more than a restaurant chain—it became a platform for living out God's plan, showing that integrity and purpose can lead to something far greater than personal success.

Mickey Robinson:

Few stories illustrate the power of God's plan more than that of my close friend Mickey Robinson. As a young skydiver, Mickey's life changed in an instant when his plane crashed, leaving him severely burned and disabled. Doctors gave him little hope, and by all accounts, his future seemed shattered. But God had a different plan. Instead of allowing his circumstances to define him,

Mickey experienced a miraculous recovery—one that defied medical expectations. His near-death experience led him into a deep encounter with God, transforming his pain into a powerful testimony. What could have kept him small and broken became the very thing that launched him into a global ministry, touching millions with his story of faith, healing, and redemption. His life is a testament that no setback is too great for God to turn around.

Alex Kendrick: A Dream for Christian Filmmaking

Alex Kendrick's journey into filmmaking was not just about storytelling; it was a divine calling, a dream God put in their hearts, to impact lives through faith-based cinema. Raised in Georgia, he first served in ministry as an associate pastor, where his passion for media and ministry merged. It was in Sherwood Baptist Church that his vision for film was ignited. Instead of waiting for Hollywood to create Christian stories, he and his brother, Stephen Kendrick, stepped forward to produce films that spoke directly to the heart of believers.

From humble beginnings with *Flywheel* (2003), a story about integrity, to *Facing the Giants* (2006), a football drama centered on trusting God amidst adversity, the Kendrick brothers crafted narratives that resonated deeply with audiences. Their success was not just measured in box office numbers, but in testimonies of lives transformed.

As their vision grew, they tackled themes of marriage restoration in *Fireproof* (2008), biblical fatherhood in *Courageous* (2011), and the power of prayer in *War Room* (2015). With each production, their films carried a core message: Faith is not passive; it is a force that reshapes lives.

Their work reflects the heart of a spiritual movement, a reminder that ministry can extend beyond pulpits and churches. Their films not only entertain but challenge viewers to step deeper into their faith, embrace leadership, and strengthen families. The Kendrick brothers' legacy is more than storytelling; it is a blueprint for faith-driven creativity, proving that when God calls, He equips. Starting with no resources but a dream. As they took steps of faith and worked their plan, God blessed them, and today their films have touched the world.

Dream and Purpose:

God still speaks today. He speaks through the Bible, in the heart, through leaders, our spouse, and in many ways. If you are asking God, "What do you want me to do?" He will get the message through to you.

Nathan the Producer:

A man in our church had spent years working in construction, helping his father run the family construction business. He loved the work, but deep inside, he felt a growing pull toward media. He knew it was more than just an interest—it was his calling. His dream was to impact the world for Jesus through media.

Determined to pursue his passion, he took online courses, sharpened his skills, and practiced relentlessly for years before ever earning a dollar. Then, one day, he was asked to film a wedding. He poured his heart into the project, producing it in a unique way. People loved his work. Word spread quickly across the region. Soon, opportunities poured in, and he found himself unable to keep up with both construction and his media business.

After much prayer, he made the difficult decision—stepping away from construction to fully embrace the media world. He knew God was calling him deeper. It was a leap of faith, but he faced his fears and stepped forward. Today, his work is seen across the world, as he produces both secular and Christian media.

Recently, he traveled with me to the remote villages of Burundi, Africa—one of the world's poorest nations, where we ministered for several weeks. He captured hours of powerful footage: tribal Pygmy people giving their hearts to Jesus, lives being touched by God in ways beyond words. The videos are raw, captivating, and filled with undeniable power. He produced a Christian documentary that tells the story of faith moving in places few have seen. The name of the film is "Light in the Darkness."

Understanding God's Timing:

One of the greatest struggles people face is waiting. God's plan often unfolds slower than we expect, and in that waiting period, doubt creeps in.

Moses waited 40 years in the desert before stepping into leadership. Joseph waited 13 years in slavery and prison before his dream became reality. David waited decades after being anointed king before he took the throne over all Israel.

Waiting doesn't mean God has forgotten you—it means He is preparing you.

> Galatians 6:9 reminds us: *"Let us not become weary in doing good, for at the proper time we will reap a harvest if we do not give up."*

Overcoming Distractions and Detours:

Sometimes, we feel off track—like we missed our purpose. But God is an expert at rerouting.

Consider Tim Tebow, the Heisman Trophy-winning quarterback. His NFL career was cut short, but instead of feeling defeated, he pivoted—becoming a speaker, author, and advocate for missions. God had a bigger plan than just football.

Another example is Joyce Meyer—before she became a world-renowned Bible teacher, she struggled with abuse and brokenness. But God redeemed her story and now uses her voice to heal millions.

- Genesis 50:20: "You intended to harm me, but God intended it for good to accomplish what is now being done, the saving of many lives."
- Romans 8:28: "And we know that in all things God works for the good of those who love him, who have been called according to his purpose."

A Personal Journey of Purpose:

For years, I was a businessman, focused on growing and sustaining a company. But God had another plan—one I couldn't see at the time. My wife and I both came from small towns, places where big dreams often seemed out of reach. We had no great resources, no obvious connections, but what we did have was the grace of God and a dream in our hearts.

God placed mentors in our lives, people who shaped our faith and helped expand our vision. Without them, we may have stayed trapped in small dreams, never realizing the depth of our calling.

Their encouragement and wisdom helped us see ourselves in a new and healthy way, not as limited, but as called and capable. Today, we have pastored for nearly 20 years, ministered in about 15 countries, and continually thank God for the people who pushed us beyond our fears and into His purpose.

God doesn't design anyone to be small and insignificant. His plan is not just for personal success or wealth, but for impact—to bless your family, and to touch the world for His good. If you feel stuck, if you question whether you were meant for more, hear this truth: You were made for a divine purpose, and that purpose is bigger than you think. He wants you to birth your dreams.

Aligning with His purpose:

So, how do you step into God's plan for your life?

1. Seek Him First (Proverbs 3:5-6) – Surrender your plans and trust that God knows better.
2. Ask Him to reveal His plan for you.
3. Write it down. Clarify it and build a plan.
4. Activate Your Faith (James 2:17) – A dream without action is wasted. Step forward, even when you don't see the whole picture.
5. Use Your Gifts (Romans 12:6-8) – Your skills and passions were given for a reason—use them boldly.
6. Don't Fear Failure (Isaiah 41:10) – Failure is not final—God uses setbacks for comebacks.
7. Never quit! Push through until you birth the vision.

Your Future is Waiting:

God's plan for your life is not ordinary—it is extraordinary. It won't always be easy, and it may not look the way you expect, but one thing is certain: If you trust Him and walk in obedience, you will step into the life you were created for.

Small Group Discussion Guide

Small Group Discussion – Chapter 2: *God Has a Dream and Purpose for Your Life*

Key Scripture: Jeremiah 29:11 (NIV)
"'For I know the plans I have for you,' declares the Lord, 'plans to prosper you and not to harm you, plans to give you hope and a future.'"

Icebreaker Question:

Ask the group, "What do you believe your personal calling is?"

Discussion Questions

1. What part of this chapter stood out to you most—and why? Was there a story, scripture, or example that spoke directly to your current season?
2. Which of the three purposes (serving God, serving others, personal calling) feels strongest in your life right now—and which one needs more focus?
   How do you think they all work together?
3. Have you ever confused a personal dream with God's purpose?
   How can we tell the difference between good ideas and God ideas?
4. Talk about a season when you had to wait on God's timing. What helped you stay faithful and hopeful during that time?

5. What "mission field" are you currently in? How can you better serve God and others right where you are (job, school, home, etc.)?
6. What is one step you can take this week to align your life more closely with God's purpose?

Prayer Focus

Take a few moments to pray for each other. Ask God to:
- Reveal His specific plan and calling.
- Rekindle dreams that may have died.
- Give courage to take the next step.
- Remove fear of failure or comparison.
- Bless each person's current "mission field."

CHAPTER 3

THE POWER OF VISION: SEE IT BEFORE YOU BUILD IT!

"Vision without action is merely a dream. Action without vision just passes the time. Vision with action can change the world."

—Joel A. Barker

Vision is the ability to see beyond the present—to grasp a future that is greater than what currently exists. It is the driving force behind success, the foundation of leadership, and the key to fulfilling purpose. Without vision, people wander aimlessly, but with vision, they move forward with clarity and determination.

Dr. Myles Munroe, a renowned teacher on leadership and purpose, often emphasized that vision is the key to unlocking destiny. He taught that God gives vision to guide people toward their purpose, and that without vision, life lacks direction.

Imagine a man deciding to build a house. He is eager, motivated, and ready to begin. But there's one problem—he has no blueprint, no design, no clear plan. He starts construction, but as the walls rise, he realizes mistakes were made. The foundation isn't strong, the rooms are uneven, and parts of the structure must be torn down and rebuilt. What should have been a dream home becomes a frustrating, unstable project—all because there was no vision to guide the process.

Now, picture a business owner launching a company with no defined plan. He has passion but no direction. His operations are chaotic, his finances are disorganized, and his goals shift constantly. Customers come and go, but nothing feels stable. Eventually, the stress, inefficiency, and lack of structure cause the business to collapse—not because the idea was bad, but because there was no clear vision driving it forward.

A church without vision faces a similar challenge. Leadership is uncertain, ministries lack focus, and members feel disconnected. Instead of moving toward a defined mission, they simply hope things will improve over time. But hope without action is not a strategy—without vision, the church struggles to grow, leaving its purpose undefined and its impact minimal.

The Power of Vision

Vision is not just wishful thinking—it is a clear mental picture of the future that inspires action. Dr. Myles Munroe described vision as:

"A mental picture of your future. It is the unveiling of God's plan for your life."

Vision is what separates:

- Leaders from followers – Those with vision chart a course while others simply react to circumstances.
- Innovators from imitators – Visionaries create opportunities rather than just copying existing ideas.
- Achievers from dreamers – Dreams remain abstract unless vision fuels action.

When vision is present, clarity replaces confusion, strategy replaces uncertainty, and momentum replaces stagnation. Vision brings purpose, and with it comes direction, discipline, and breakthrough.

Quotes on Vision:

- *"Vision is the Source and hope of life. The greatest gift ever given to mankind is not the gift of sight, but the gift of vision. Sight is a function of the eyes; vision is a function of the heart. 'Eyes that look are common, but eyes that see are rare.' Nothing noble or noteworthy on earth was ever done without vision."*—Myles Munroe
- *"Leadership is the capacity to influence others through inspiration motivated by passion, generated by vision, produced by a conviction, ignited by a purpose."*—Myles M.
- *"Purpose is when you know and understand what you were born to accomplish. Vision is when you can see it in your mind and begin to imagine it."*—Myles Munroe
- *"Where there is no vision, the people perish."*—Proverbs 29:18
- *"The only thing worse than being blind is having sight but no vision."* –Helen Keller

- *"A dream without a plan is just a wish."*—Antoine de Saint-Exupéry
- *"You must see it before you build it!"*—Bob Pittman

Biblical Examples of Visionaries

The Bible is filled with leaders who changed history because they had vision—a divine sense of purpose that drove them forward despite obstacles, doubts, and opposition. Their ability to see beyond the present challenges and focus on God's greater plan sets them apart as transformational figures.

1. Joseph's Vision of Leadership (Genesis 37:5-11).
    - Joseph had a dream that he would lead, but his journey was filled with obstacles. His vision kept him focused through betrayal, slavery, and imprisonment, until he finally became a ruler in Egypt. He was then entrusted to create a plan to save all of Egypt.
2. Nehemiah's Vision to Rebuild Jerusalem (Nehemiah 2:5-8).
    - Nehemiah saw the ruins of Jerusalem and envisioned its restoration. He developed a plan, gathered resources, and led the rebuilding effort, proving that vision requires action and strategy.
3. Jesus' Vision for the Kingdom of God (Luke 4:18-19).
    - Jesus had a clear vision—to bring salvation to the world. His vision guided His ministry, and He trained His disciples to carry that vision forward. Jesus taught 12 men how to win and disciple. Through this model, Christianity has become the largest religion in the world.

Visionary Leaders in Business and Ministry:

Many successful leaders have mastered the art of vision, turning ideas into reality. Their ability to see beyond the present, anticipate the future, and take decisive action has shaped industries, movements, and even history. Visionary leaders don't simply react to circumstances—they create opportunities, inspire others, and drive change.

- They see potential where others see obstacles: Instead of being discouraged by challenges, visionary leaders embrace them as stepping stones toward something greater.
- They think long-term: Vision isn't just about immediate success; it's about building something lasting, something that impacts generations.
- They inspire action: A true leader's vision is contagious. They motivate others to believe, work toward a goal, and contribute to a bigger purpose.
- They adapt and innovate: Visionaries don't stay stagnant; they adjust, evolve, and refine their ideas to meet changing realities.

Examples of Visionaries: How Vision Transformed Industries and Ministries:

Visionaries don't just see what exists; they see what could be. They recognize problems, anticipate future needs, and take bold steps to turn ideas into reality. Their ability to develop and implement vision has led to tremendous success and lasting impact.

1. Sam Walton (Walmart Founder)

When Sam Walton looked at retail, he saw a flawed system—stores that were either overpriced or inefficient. He envisioned a better way—a store that could provide affordable, high-quality products to everyday families without sacrificing service or selection.

Instead of following the traditional retail model, Walton disrupted the industry by pioneering a low-cost, high-volume approach. He focused on cutting costs, optimizing supply chains, and strategically opening stores in small towns—places many competitors overlooked. His vision wasn't just about selling products; it was about changing the way people shop.

The result? Walmart became the largest retailer in the world, proving that vision paired with strategy and execution can revolutionize an industry.

2. Reed Hastings (Netflix CEO)

In the late 1990s, video rentals were dominated by Blockbuster's physical stores, where late fees frustrated customers. Hastings saw a better future—one where people could watch movies anytime, anywhere, without the hassle of renting and returning discs.

Netflix started as a DVD rental-by-mail service, which was innovative at the time. But Hastings wasn't just thinking about DVDs—he anticipated the shift toward digital streaming, long before it was mainstream. When most companies dismissed the idea, he invested heavily in content licensing, technology, and original programming.

The result? Netflix became a global streaming powerhouse, transforming how people consume entertainment. His vision forced Hollywood to adapt, ushering in the era of on-demand content and shaking up the industry forever.

3. Billy Graham (Evangelist)

Billy Graham saw a spiritual need—people were hungry for truth, yet few evangelistic efforts reached the masses effectively. He envisioned a way to share the Gospel on a global scale, using mass media, strategic outreach, and large-scale gatherings.

His crusades weren't just local church revivals; they were massive events, planned with precision, supported by networks of churches, and broadcast to millions. Graham didn't settle for traditional methods—he harnessed radio, television, and eventually the internet, ensuring that his message reached far beyond the physical locations of his crusades.

The result? Millions came to Christ, and Graham became one of the most influential evangelists of all time. His vision reshaped Christian outreach, showing that strategic planning and faith could bring revival across nations.

4. Rick Warren (Saddleback Church)

Rick Warren saw a common struggle in churches—believers were attending services but lacked clear direction for their spiritual growth. He envisioned a purpose-driven ministry, one where people understood their God-given calling and lived with intentionality.

Warren didn't just preach sermons; he developed a structured framework—one that guided churches and individuals toward spiritual growth, service, and mission. His book, *The Purpose-Driven*

Life, became a global bestseller, influencing not just churches but leaders across industries.

The result? Saddleback Church grew into a thriving ministry, and thousands of churches worldwide adopted purpose-driven strategies, shifting from passive attendance to active engagement in faith.

The Power of Vision:

Each of these leaders recognized a need, envisioned a solution, and executed a plan. Their vision wasn't just a dream—it was a strategic force that reshaped industries, churches, and individual lives.

Vision isn't just about seeing the future—it's about building it.

How to Develop a Powerful Vision:

If you want to fulfill your dream, you must develop a clear, focused vision. Vision is the bridge between your present and your purpose; it's what keeps you moving when life gets difficult. A God-given vision provides direction, discipline, and motivation. Below are steps to build a dynamic vision.

- Seek God's Guidance (Proverbs 3:5–6) – Vision doesn't begin with ambition; it begins with surrender. Ask God to reveal His plan for your life. Trust that He knows what's best and wants to guide you. Prayer, fasting, and time in the Word will sharpen your spiritual clarity.
- Write It Down (Habakkuk 2:2) – Don't just think about it—document it. Writing your vision makes it tangible and gives it structure. A written vision becomes a compass

that keeps you aligned, focused, and intentional. It is also a practice to write out a one-year, five-year, and twenty-year vision.

- Ask Yourself: What Do You Really Want to Do?
  Dig deep and get specific. What do you feel called to build, lead, create, or change? Who do you want to impact? If you could do anything without fear, what would it be? Be honest—clarity is power.
- Break It Into Steps – Big vision without clear steps becomes overwhelming. Divide your vision into goals, and your goals into actions. What can you do this week, this month, or this year to move closer? Faith without a plan can become frustration.
- Visualize the Outcome – Use your imagination in faith. See yourself walking in your calling. Picture the lives impacted, the doors opened, and the transformation God will bring through you. What you can see, you can begin to pursue.
- Surround Yourself with Visionaries (Proverbs 27:17) – You become like those you spend time with. Stay close to people who dream big, think forward, and live with purpose. Their momentum will stir your own.
- Take Action – Vision without movement is just a dream. Start now. Take the first step, no matter how small. Progress is made by those who are willing to act in faith before everything is perfect.
- Revisit and Refine the Vision – Vision is not a one-time revelation; it evolves as you grow. Stay close to God and allow Him to refine and expand your vision over time.

Considerations When Building a Business Vision:

Creating a strong business vision requires clarity, strategy, and alignment with your values. Here are some key elements to consider:

- Purpose Beyond Profit
  Ask: *Why does this business exist beyond making money?* A business with a clear mission serves customers, solves problems, and makes a lasting impact. Profit is a byproduct of purpose-driven excellence.
- Identify the Target Audience or Customer
  Know who you're serving. What are their needs, challenges, and desires? A clear vision should speak directly to the people you are called to reach.
- Solve a Specific Problem
  Great businesses are built around solutions. What pain point are you addressing? Clarity around this will shape your products, services, and messaging.
- Core Values and Culture
  Define the principles that will guide your team and brand. These values create the atmosphere in which your business will operate and attract like-minded people.
- Scalability and Sustainability
  Think long-term. Can your vision grow? Will it still be effective and profitable five or ten years from now? Build with the future in mind.
- Adaptability in Changing Markets
  A strong vision must be flexible. How will you stay relevant as technology, trends, and needs shift? Vision should be strong in purpose but adaptable in method.

- Integration of Faith and Ethics
  For faith-based entrepreneurs, consider how biblical values shape leadership, decision-making, and service. Integrity and excellence should be at the core.

In-N-Out Burger Example:

In-N-Out Burger is a well-known example of a business that has quietly but intentionally woven Christian faith into its vision and operations. Founded in 1948 by Harry and Esther Snyder, the company has remained privately owned and family-run, allowing it to maintain its original values. Faith became more visibly integrated under the leadership of their son, Rich Snyder, who was a devout Christian. Today, In-N-Out includes subtle yet powerful reminders of its faith-based roots, such as Bible verse references printed on the bottom of cups and wrappers (e.g., John 3:16 on drink cups). While the company doesn't advertise itself as a Christian business, its commitment to integrity, quality, and treating employees with respect all reflect a vision shaped by biblical principles. In-N-Out demonstrates that it's possible to build a successful, large-scale company while remaining true to spiritual convictions.

Considerations When Building a Ministry Vision:

A ministry vision must be birthed in prayer, anchored in Scripture, and directed by the Holy Spirit. Here's what to keep in mind:

- God's Calling and Timing
  What has God specifically called you to do? Ministry begins with divine assignment, not personal ambition. Wait on His direction—then move in obedience.

- Define the Core Mission

  What is the spiritual purpose of this ministry? Is it evangelism, discipleship, outreach, healing, teaching, or leadership development? A clear mission creates focus.

- Know Your People

  Who are you called to reach? Understand the demographic, spiritual condition, and needs of your audience. What problems are you solving? Ministry is most effective when it meets people where they are.

- Biblical Foundation

  Every ministry must be built on the truth of God's Word. Your vision should align with Scripture and reflect the heart of Jesus in both message and method.

- Spirit-led Strategy

  Vision without spiritual direction becomes human effort. Seek the Holy Spirit's guidance for both short-term steps and long-term goals.

- Leadership Structure and Accountability

  Ministry must have healthy leadership. Who's on your team? What systems ensure accountability, stewardship, and alignment with the mission?

- Sustainability and Legacy

  Think beyond your own role—can this ministry thrive after you? Are you raising up future leaders and building something that lasts?

- Community Impact

  Your ministry shouldn't just live inside the four walls—it should transform communities. Consider how your vision will bring healing, hope, and spiritual awakening to the surrounding area.

Strategy in Ministry:

In a Christian ministry, strategy is essential to turning vision into action. A God-given vision will always involve people—reaching them, serving them, and leading them into deeper relationship with Christ. But without strategy, even the most powerful vision remains an idea rather than a movement. Ministries must prayerfully develop clear, actionable plans that answer the question: *How are we going to reach the people God has called us to serve?*

Here are some key strategic components for Christian ministry:

- Small Groups – One of the most effective ministry strategies, small groups foster discipleship, accountability, and authentic community. Jesus Himself modeled this by spending most of His ministry with a small group of twelve. Ministries can multiply their impact by raising up leaders and creating environments for people to grow in faith and relationship with others. Healthy small group ministry should also be missional. To foster an environment where people invite their friends to the group to ultimately see them born again.
- Outreach and Service Projects – Strategic outreach involves going *outside the walls* of the church to meet people where they are. This might include feeding programs, block parties, school partnerships, prison ministry, or neighborhood clean-ups—each one a way to show the love of Christ in action.
- Targeted Ministry Tracks – Create specific strategies for different groups: children, youth, young adults, families,

men, women, and seniors. Tailor teaching, mentorship, and events to address their unique needs and life stages.
- Digital Strategy – In today's world, digital platforms are mission fields. Live-streaming services, social media ministry, and podcasting allow the church to reach far beyond its local setting. A strong online presence is no longer optional—it's part of fulfilling the Great Commission.
- Leadership Development – A visionary ministry equips and multiplies leaders. Develop training systems that raise up future pastors, small group leaders, and ministry directors who can carry the vision forward with excellence and spiritual maturity.
- Prayer Strategy – Vision without prayer is powerless. Build a culture of prayer throughout the ministry—prayer meetings, intercessory teams, and intentional prayer coverage for services and outreach initiatives. This ensures that every part of the strategy is rooted in God's direction and strength.

Ultimately, the strategy must reflect the heart of the vision: to make disciples, transform lives, and glorify God. A Spirit-led strategy bridges the gap between dreaming and doing—turning the vision into a living, breathing ministry that changes communities for the Kingdom.

Your Vision Determines Your Future:

Vision is the roadmap to destiny. Without it, people drift—but with it, they thrive. If you want to step into your calling, you must see beyond today and move toward the future with purpose.

"Vision without action is merely a dream. Action without vision just passes the time. Vision with action can change the world."

—Joel A. Barker

Are you ready to embrace the power of vision?

Small Group Lesson – The Power of Vision

Title: *See it Before You Build it!*

Key Verse: *"Where there is no vision, the people perish."*
— Proverbs 29:18 (KJV)

Big Idea:

Vision is a clear, God-inspired picture of the future that compels us to take action. Without vision, people and organizations drift—but with vision, lives are transformed.

Icebreaker:

If you could build *anything* with unlimited resources, what would you build and why?

Scripture Focus:

1. Genesis 37:5–11 – Joseph's dream and the obstacles he faced.
2. Nehemiah 2:5–8 – Nehemiah's strategic request to rebuild Jerusalem.
3. Habakkuk 2:2-3 – Write the vision and make it plain.

Discussion Questions:

- What do these stories teach us about the power of vision?

- How did each person align their vision with God's purpose?
- What obstacles did they overcome by keeping vision alive?

Key Quote for Reflection:

"Vision is the source and hope of life . . . Sight is a function of the eyes; vision is a function of the heart."

—Dr. Myles Munroe

Group Discussion:

1. Have you ever pursued something without a clear vision? What was the outcome?
2. What's one area of your life (business, ministry, family, etc.) that needs clearer vision?
3. What might God be showing you about your future?

Practical Application:

Take a Vision Step:
Give each group member a notecard and ask them to write down answers to the following:
- What do I believe God is calling me to build or lead?
- What's one small step I can take this week to begin?

Encourage them to:

- Pray daily for clarity.

- Share their vision with one trusted person for encouragement.
- Write down a 1-year or 5-year vision.

Closing Prayer:

Pray that God would open the eyes of each member's heart, give clarity, and ignite bold action. Ask for courage to take the first step toward their God-given purpose.

Optional Challenge:

Read the book of Nehemiah this week—journal every time Nehemiah shows vision, planning, and prayer.

CHAPTER 4

FAITH: MOVE MOUNTAINS

"Never be afraid to trust an unknown future to a known God."

—Corrie ten Boom

Faith is the bridge between where you are and where God is leading you. It's the force that moves mountains, opens doors, and turns impossibilities into testimonies. Throughout history, both in the Bible and in modern times, people have faced moments of being stuck, times when their dreams seemed unreachable, their circumstances overwhelming, and their future uncertain. But faith in God changed everything.

"Faith opens our eyes to a new kind of vision and gives us the light of God to see by."

— C.S. Lewis

For years, I worked in the software industry—and I loved it. I was constantly traveling, always on a plane headed somewhere new. I helped design products, build marketing strategies, and close major business deals. As a young man, that fast-paced life brought me a deep sense of fulfillment.

What most people didn't see, though, was what was happening behind the scenes. I was learning to apply faith in every step of my journey. Faith became a driving force—not just a belief, but a practical tool that helped me move forward. And I discovered that it truly makes a difference. God, through faith, can help you fulfill your dreams.

One day, I received a call from my business partner. He had closed a very large software deal several months earlier with a food distribution company. I thought everything was going well. However, he informed me that the lead engineer had completely dropped the ball and then quit our company. We were months behind on their project, and what they had received was not working. The customer called and said they were going to sue us. The situation was very serious and could have cost the company hundreds of thousands of dollars. My partner said, "I know this isn't your issue, but I need you to resolve this quickly." I hung up the phone, closed my office door, and prayed. I felt a deep peace come over me. The voice of the Lord spoke in my heart, "Trust Me."

I set up an appointment to visit the company. I prepared well for the meeting and spent much time in prayer, asking God for His wisdom and guidance. Again, the inner voice of God echoed, "Trust Me." When I was pulling into the parking lot of their company, I had a supernatural encounter. A deep impression filled my heart. Without words, the Holy Spirit said, "Meet with them, be confident but humble, let them fully vent their frustrations, take a lunch break, and then have a final meeting to resolve all issues."

I met with about 25 people in a large meeting room, including a lawyer, department heads, engineers, and the president of the company. I took control of the meeting and asked them to go around the table and vent any frustrations regarding the project. I was met with much anger, tone, threats, and belittling comments. I took notes, and after 90 minutes, we took a lunch break. It was ugly. I skipped lunch and thought I would organize my thoughts and spend a few minutes in needed prayer. I wasn't sure this was going well, but I knew the Lord was with me.

As I sat in the conference room, I decided to check my email. Wouldn't you know it, a missionary friend sent me some pictures from a South American mission's trip. People were at the altar crying in the picture. Then a voice behind me spoke, "What is that?" I turned and looked; it was the president of the company. I smiled and said, "I'm a Christian, and this is one of the places I visited on a missionary trip." His eyes filled with tears, and he turned his head to shield the emotion. Then he stared at me and said, "I used to do the same with YWAM. I have grown so cold. I need to get my life right again." Then he left the room.

My heart was swimming with thoughts. I knew this was a set-up from heaven. Soon, all the people began to fill the room. The company's president walked in late with some papers. He interrupted the meeting and said, "I trust this man. I do. I trust him. We are going to give him an opportunity to fix this mess. As a sign of my commitment, I have an additional purchase order for $58,000 to expand our systems." Everyone groaned and stared at me. I thanked him, dismissed all the business personnel, and worked out a plan with the engineers. We held true to our commitment and completed their system to their satisfaction.

This was not luck; this was faith in action. I had no recourse but to firmly trust God. Faith is a necessity in business and ministry.

Wigglesworth Bible

Several years ago, I received a priceless gift—a Bible that once belonged to the great faith evangelist, Smith Wigglesworth. It was given to me by dear family friends, Morice and Esther Oleson, both of whom are now with the Lord. Esther's father, Arthur Vourie, was a close friend and translator for Smith Wigglesworth during the 1930s.

As a young man, I often stayed in their home. During those visits, they would fill my heart with powerful stories—accounts of miracles, faith, and encounters from both Smith's ministry and their own. Their home was filled with photos and articles that documented it all. (One day, I'll share those stories in another book.)

I'll never forget the moment something inside me shifted. As I listened to their stories, a deep stirring began in my heart—what I can only describe as a fire of faith being kindled. It wasn't just inspiration; it was as if God Himself was inviting me into a life of true faith, a partnership with Him for the impossible.

Even now, I sometimes hold Smith's Bible during my morning prayer time. It serves as a tangible reminder of what's possible when we choose to believe God. Smith Wigglesworth's life remains a powerful testimony of how faith can transform the ordinary into the miraculous.

What is faith?

Faith is the currency of the Kingdom of God. It is the invisible force that brings heaven's reality to the earth. Without faith, nothing moves in the spiritual realm—because faith is what pleases God (Hebrews 11:6). It is not just belief in God's existence; it is trust in His nature, confidence in His promises, and boldness to act on His Word.

Jesus taught us that faith is powerful, active, and able to move mountains. And able to assist you in fulfilling your dream. Jesus said: "If you have faith as small as a mustard seed, you can say to this mountain, 'Move from here to there,' and it will move. Nothing will be impossible for you" (Matthew 17:20 NIV).

Biblical Definition of Faith:

> "Now faith is the substance of things hoped for, the evidence of things not seen."
>
> —*Hebrews 11:1 (NKJV)*

Faith is not wishful thinking. It is the **substance**—the spiritual foundation—of what we hope for. It's the **evidence** of things we can't yet see. Faith reaches into the unseen and pulls the promises of God into our present reality.

Faith is Believing, Speaking, and Acting

Faith doesn't sit still. It believes, it speaks, and it moves. Paul said:

> "We believe, therefore we speak."
>
> – *2 Corinthians 4:13 (NIV)*

> True faith speaks the Word of God in agreement with His will. It also takes action based on that belief. James put it this way: "Faith by itself, if it does not have works, is dead."
>
> – *James 2:17 (NKJV)*

Do All Believers Have Faith?

Yes! Every believer has been given a measure of faith. "...God has dealt to each one a measure of faith" (Romans 12:3 NKJV).

We may not all be at the same level of faith maturity, but we all start with the same God-given measure. The apostles didn't receive "special" faith—they *developed* their faith by walking closely with Jesus, stepping out in obedience, and trusting the Father.

You can grow your faith the same way: by hearing the Word (Romans 10:17), obeying the promptings of the Holy Spirit, and exercising your faith through action.

As Smith Wigglesworth once said, "Fear looks, faith jumps. Faith never fails to obtain. If I leave you as I found you, I'm not God's channel. I'm not here to entertain you, but to get you to the place where you can laugh at the impossible."

Faith is not reserved for a few elite Christians. Anyone who is in right relationship with God can walk by faith and see the supernatural released. Jesus made this promise to all who believe:

> "Whoever believes in Me will do the works I have been doing, and they will do even greater things than these..."
> – John 14:12 NIV

Quotes from Faith Generals:

- Kenneth Hagin: "Faith begins where the will of God is known."
- Oral Roberts: "Something good is going to happen to you today if you'll believe."
- Catherine Booth: "Faith is not an emotion; it is a principle."

- Lester Sumrall: "Feed your faith and starve your doubts to death."

Faith is a Lifestyle

Faith is not a moment—it's a **way of life**. Paul wrote: "The just shall live by faith"

– Romans 1:17 KJV

If you're right with God, then you're called to live by faith. You don't need to wait for more signs, feelings, or perfect conditions. You already have what you need to walk in faith and see God move.

"Only believe."

– Jesus, Mark 5:36

Biblical Stories of Faith in Hard Times:

The Bible is filled with stories of people who were stuck—trapped by circumstances, fear, or opposition—but faith in God led them to victory.

1. Abraham's Faith in God's Promise (Genesis 15:6): Abraham was old, and his wife Sarah was barren. Yet, God promised him descendants as numerous as the stars. Despite every natural limitation, Abraham believed—and God fulfilled His promise.
2. Joseph's Journey from Prison to Power (Genesis 37-50): Betrayed by his brothers, sold into slavery, falsely accused, and imprisoned—Joseph had every reason to give up. But he held onto faith, trusting that God had a

greater plan. In time, he rose to power in Egypt and saved nations from famine.

3. Moses Leading Israel Through the Red Sea (Exodus 14): Trapped between Pharaoh's army and the Red Sea, Israel had no way out. But Moses trusted God, stretched out his staff, and the waters parted. What seemed impossible became a miracle.

4. David Facing Goliath (1 Samuel 17): A young shepherd boy stood before a giant warrior. Logic said he would lose, but faith said otherwise. With a single stone, David defeated Goliath, proving that faith in God is greater than any obstacle.

5. The Woman with the Issue of Blood (Mark 5:25-34): She had suffered for 12 years, spent all her money on doctors, and found no cure. But one touch of Jesus' garment changed everything. Her faith brought healing when nothing else could.

As we read about many of the heroes of the faith, we learn that they had a precious gift. This gift allowed them to build from nothing and create a healthy, thriving ministry. The key to each of these was simple yet powerful faith.

- Billy Graham Evangelistic Association: Billy Graham began preaching in small churches with no budget before reaching millions worldwide. He did this through trusting God with the budget, attendance, and large crusades.
- Mother Teresa's Missionaries of Charity: Started with a single mission to serve the poor in Calcutta, now a global movement.

- Reinhard Bonnke's Christ for All Nations: Began with small, low-budget crusades, later drawing millions to Christ across Africa.
- T.L. Osborn Ministries: Started with little to no resources but became a worldwide evangelistic force.

Faith-Based Organizations that Changed the World:

- **World Vision**: Founded by Bob Pierce with a heart for helping children in poverty.
- **Samaritan's Purse**: Franklin Graham expanded this ministry to provide disaster relief globally. It started with a simple vision.
- **Compassion International**: Started small but now sponsors millions of children worldwide.

These individuals and organizations prove that **faith, vision, and perseverance** can transform lives and impact generations.

Faith in Action: The Story of William Colgate

Faith is more than belief—it's a force that shapes lives, transforms businesses, and turns humble beginnings into legacies. Few stories illustrate this better than that of William Colgate, the founder of Colgate-Palmolive.

Colgate was born in England in 1783 and immigrated to America in 1798 with his family. With little to his name, he took an apprenticeship in soap-making, a trade that would eventually define his life's work. But before success, he faced failure—his first business venture collapsed. Many might have given up, but Colgate leaned on Scripture, prayer, and wise counsel, choosing faith over fear.

Inspired by Genesis 28:20-21, where Jacob vowed to give a tenth of his earnings to God, Colgate committed to tithing from his first income. His soap business slowly gained traction, expanding beyond local sales and ultimately growing into a global corporation.

As his wealth increased, Colgate did not hoard his success—he shared it. His commitment to tithing deepened as he began giving away 50% of his income to Bible societies, missionary work, and theological education. His business thrived, not only because of strategy and hard work but because he honored God first.

Colgate's story is a testament to faith-driven perseverance. He didn't wait for perfect conditions—he worked with what he had, trusted God, and remained generous. His name is now synonymous with one of the largest consumer goods companies in the world, but his greatest legacy is not toothpaste—it is faith in action.

What dream or business are you pursuing? Let Colgate's story remind you: Faith, combined with action, builds legacies.

Modern Stories of Faith in Business and Life:

Faith isn't just a biblical concept. It is a gift God gives us. True faith has shaped the lives of countless leaders, entrepreneurs, and visionaries.

Dave Thomas – Founder of Wendy's:

Before Wendy's became a household name, Dave Thomas faced poverty and rejection. He was adopted, struggled in school, and worked tirelessly in the restaurant industry. But faith and perseverance led him to build one of the most successful fast-food chains in history.

On a side note. His Christian faith also impacted him in the area of servanthood. He would tell the franchise owners and staff to get an "M.B.A.", which in this case didn't stand for Master of Business Administration but instead stood for "mop bucket attitude." Meaning, be a servant to the customer and the organization.

Blake Mycoskie – Founder of TOMS Shoes:

On a trip to Argentina, Blake saw children without shoes. Instead of ignoring the problem, he stepped out in faith, launching a company that donates a pair of shoes for every pair sold. His business model, built on faith and generosity, has impacted millions.

Peter Rex – CEO of Rex LLC:

Peter Rex built a real estate and technology empire, but his journey wasn't easy. He faced financial struggles, setbacks, and uncertainty. Yet, his faith-driven leadership helped him push forward, proving that business success and Christian values can go hand in hand. His company is built on the idea that businesses should serve people, not just generate wealth.

Mart Green – Founder of Mardel Christian & Education:

As the son of Hobby Lobby's founder, Mart Green had a vision to create a faith-based retail chain. He faced challenges in launching and sustaining the business, but his faith in God and commitment to biblical principles led to success.

Mary Kay Ash - the founder of Mary Kay Inc:

Mary Kay Ash started her cosmetics company in 1963 with a simple but powerful mission—to empower women while honoring God. She built her business on Christian values, prioritizing faith, integrity, and servant leadership.

One of her guiding principles was, "God first, family second, career third," which shaped the culture of her company. She encouraged employees and sales consultants to lead with kindness, generosity, and ethical business practices. Despite facing skepticism as a female entrepreneur in a male-dominated industry, she relied on her faith to push forward.

Her commitment to biblical values helped Mary Kay Inc. grow into one of the largest direct-selling beauty brands in the world, proving that faith-driven leadership can lead to both business success and lasting impact.

Robert G. LeTourneau – God's Businessman:

Few entrepreneurs embodied faith-driven success like Robert G. LeTourneau. A sixth-grade dropout, LeTourneau faced financial struggles, setbacks, and uncertainty throughout his early career. At one point, he was $100,000 in debt during the Great Depression, a situation that could have permanently crushed his business.

But instead of giving up, LeTourneau sought God's guidance. He believed that God needed businessmen, too, and he committed to running his company as a partnership with God. His faith led him to innovate, securing over 300 patents and revolutionizing the earth-moving equipment industry.

Despite his success, LeTourneau remained deeply committed to his faith, donating 90% of his wealth to Christian causes and missions. His story proves that faith, perseverance, and a commitment to God's principles can lead to extraordinary breakthroughs—even in the toughest circumstances.

Heidi Baker – Faith in Action:

Few missionaries have demonstrated radical faith like Heidi Baker. Called to missions at the age of 16, Heidi and her husband, Rolland, founded Iris Global, a ministry that has transformed Mozambique and beyond. When they first arrived in Mozambique, they faced extreme poverty, opposition, and a lack of resources. At one point, they were given an orphanage that no one wanted—80 neglected, demon-afflicted children in rags.

Instead of turning away, Heidi trusted God completely, believing that His provision would be enough. Over time, miracles began to unfold—children were saved, healed, and filled with the Holy Spirit. The ministry expanded, reaching thousands of churches, schools, medical clinics, and orphan care centers. Today, Heidi is known as "Mama Heidi" to countless children, and her faith-driven leadership has impacted millions worldwide.

Her story is a powerful reminder that faith in God can overcome any obstacle, no matter how impossible the circumstances seem.

Taking Action: Strengthening Your Faith:

1. Speak God's Promises Over Your Life (Romans 10:17) – Faith grows by hearing and declaring God's Word.
2. Step Forward, Even When It's Uncertain (Hebrews 11:1) – Faith is confidence in what we hope for—not what we already see.

3. Surround Yourself with Faith-Filled People (Proverbs 27:17) – Iron sharpens iron. Your environment shapes your beliefs.

Your Breakthrough Begins with Faith:

No matter how stuck you feel, faith is the key to moving forward. The greatest victories in history—both biblical and modern—were won by those who refused to let fear stop them.

> Mark 9:23: "Jesus said unto him, 'If thou canst believe, all things are possible to him that believeth.'"

Small Group Lesson: Faith: Move Mountains

Key Verse:

"Now faith is the substance of things hoped for, the evidence of things not seen."

– Hebrews 11:1 (NKJV)

Opening Thought:

Faith is not just a belief—it's a bridge. It connects where you are to where God is calling you. It's the tool God gives us to overcome fear, break through limitations, and step into His promises. Faith is how we partner with God for the impossible.

Discussion Starter:

Q1: When have you had to step out in faith before you saw the outcome? What happened?

Faith Defined:

Faith is:
- Confidence in God's promises.
- Trust in His nature and Word.
- Action based on belief, not sight.

Jesus said: *"If you have faith as a mustard seed . . . nothing will be impossible for you."*

—MATTHEW 17:20

Real-Life Examples:

- Smith Wigglesworth's Bible inspired a young man (the author) to believe for miracles and live by radical faith.
- William Colgate tithed from his first paycheck and built a global business by honoring God.
- Heidi Baker believed God for provision in impossible conditions—and saw nations changed.

Group Questions:

Q2: What stood out to you from one of the faith stories in this chapter?

Q3: Do you believe faith can be developed like a muscle? How do you grow your faith personally?

Takeaway Truth:

"Faith begins where the will of God is known."

—KENNETH HAGIN

You already have a measure of faith (Romans 12:3). It's time to use it. Faith is not a moment—it's a lifestyle.

Faith in Action Challenge:

1. Speak God's promises over a specific area of your life this week. (Romans 10:17)
2. Act on something God has been prompting you to do—even if it feels risky. (James 2:17)
3. Share a story of faith this week to encourage someone else.

Prayer:

Lord, thank You for the gift of faith. Help me to trust You even when I can't see the outcome. Teach me to believe, speak, and act in faith—knowing that all things are possible when I believe. In Jesus' name, amen.

CHAPTER 5

BELIEVING IN YOURSELF – KEYS TO CONFIDENCE

"Believe you can and you're halfway there."
—Theodore Roosevelt

Confidence is one of the most powerful forces in life. It determines how you approach opportunities, how you face challenges, and ultimately, how far you'll go. But for many, confidence feels just out of reach—buried under doubt, fear, or negative experiences. The good news is that confidence isn't something you're born with—it's something you build. And when combined with faith in God, confidence can unlock doors that once seemed impossible.

The Benefits of Confidence in Business and Working with People:

Confidence is more than a personality trait—it's a spiritual and practical advantage. When rooted in Christ and guided by integrity, confidence becomes a magnet for opportunity, influence, and trust. Here are several ways confidence impacts business and relationships:

1. Confidence Builds Trust

People follow leaders who believe in what they're saying. When you carry yourself with assurance—without arrogance—others are more likely to trust your decisions, ideas, and leadership.

> "The wicked flee when no one pursues, but the righteous are bold as a lion."
>
> —Proverbs 28:1 (NKJV)

2. Confidence Accelerates Decision-Making

Indecision can stall momentum. Confidence allows you to move forward decisively, even when outcomes aren't guaranteed. In business, this can mean the difference between seizing a moment and missing it.

3. Confidence Attracts Opportunity

People are drawn to those who carry vision and conviction. Clients, investors, and team members are more likely to partner with you when you exude clarity and self-assurance.

4. Confidence Inspires Others

Your confidence can activate the courage in others. Whether you're leading a team or mentoring a friend, confidence is contagious. It lifts the atmosphere and raises the standard.

"Let your light so shine before men…"
—MATTHEW 5:16

5. Confidence Fuels Innovation

When you believe in your God-given potential, you take more creative risks. You're not paralyzed by the fear of failure. This opens doors for innovation, strategic thinking, and fresh solutions.

6. Confidence Improves Communication

Confident people speak clearly, listen actively, and present ideas effectively. In meetings, presentations, and negotiations, this often leads to stronger outcomes and deeper collaboration.

7. Confidence Reduces Fear of Rejection

You won't always get a "yes"—but confidence helps you bounce back and keep going. Rejection doesn't define you when your identity is rooted in Christ.

8. Confidence Strengthens Your Witness

In the marketplace, your boldness in who you are—and whose you are—can open spiritual conversations. People respect those who lead with consistency, humility, and unwavering belief.

"Being confident of this very thing, that He who has begun a good work in you will complete it…"
—PHILIPPIANS 1:6 (NKJV)

The Battle Against Self-Doubt

Many people struggle with self-doubt, believing they're not smart enough, talented enough, or capable enough to achieve their goals. These limiting thoughts can feel like chains, keeping people stuck in patterns of hesitation and insecurity. But here's the truth: Your potential isn't based on how others see you—it's based on how God sees you.

In Judges 6:11-16, we see Gideon—timid, uncertain, and convinced of his own inadequacy. When God called him to lead Israel, he couldn't fathom the possibility. He saw himself as weak, insignificant, and incapable of such a huge task. But God didn't see a fearful man hiding in the shadows—He saw a mighty warrior, one destined to lead a nation to victory.

Like Gideon, we often fail to recognize the gifts and talents locked up inside us. We let fear, doubt, and past failures define us, forgetting that our true identity lies in what God sees, not what we feel. Gideon had everything he needed to change the course of history, but it was buried beneath hesitation. Yet when God unlocked his confidence, Gideon became unstoppable.

The same is true for us. There is greatness within, waiting to be awakened. God has placed extraordinary purpose, strength, and wisdom inside of you—not for it to remain dormant, but for it to be released in power. When we step fully into our God-given identity, barriers fall, strongholds break, and we move forward into the destiny we were designed to fulfill.

Or think about Elon Musk, the visionary behind Tesla and SpaceX. Early in his career, Musk faced constant criticism—people said his ideas were impossible, his ambitions foolish. But instead of giving in to doubt, he chose confidence, believing that persistence could make the impossible possible. Today, he has revolutionized multiple industries.

How to Develop Self-Confidence:

Confidence isn't something you're either born with or without—it's something you build, especially when your foundation is Christ. True confidence comes from knowing who you are, whose you are, and what you're called to do. Here are practical and biblical steps to grow in self-confidence:

1. Know Your Identity in Christ

The strongest confidence comes from knowing that you are a child of God, created with purpose and value. Your worth is not based on performance but on your position in Christ.

> "For you are all sons of God through faith in Christ Jesus."
> —Galatians 3:26 (NKJV)

- Action Step: Meditate on scriptures that affirm your identity (e.g., 2 Corinthians 5:17; Romans 8:16–17).

2. Silence the Inner Critic:

Many people live with an internal voice of fear, doubt, or shame. But confidence grows when you replace that voice with God's truth.

> "Let the weak say, 'I am strong.'"
> —Joel 3:10 (NKJV)

- Action Step: Write down negative thoughts, then write God's truth next to each one. Declare His Word over your life daily.

3. Celebrate Small Wins:

Confidence builds through momentum. Every time you step out and succeed—even in something small—you strengthen your belief in what's possible.
- Action Step: At the end of each week, list three things you accomplished or did well. Celebrate progress, not perfection.

4. Do Hard Things on Purpose:

Self-confidence grows when you push past comfort. God often leads us into unfamiliar territory so that we'll depend on Him—and grow stronger.

> "Be strong and courageous . . . for the Lord your God is with you wherever you go."
>
> —Joshua 1:9 (NIV)

- Action Step: Choose one thing each week that stretches you—whether it's speaking up in a meeting, trying something new, or sharing your faith.

5. Surround Yourself with Encouragers:

Confidence is contagious. When you spend time with people who believe in you and speak life over you, your faith and boldness grow.

> "Therefore encourage one another and build each other up..."
>
> —1 Thessalonians 5:11 (NIV)

- Action Step: Identify a few "confidence-builders" in your life—mentors, friends, leaders—and stay closely connected to them.

6. Keep Showing Up:

One of the secrets to confidence is consistency. Show up. Try again. Don't quit. Over time, consistency builds competence—and competence builds confidence.

> "Do not grow weary in doing good, for in due season we will reap, if we do not give up."
>
> —Galatians 6:9 (ESV)

- Action Step: Choose one area where you've felt discouraged or unqualified and commit to show up faithfully for 30 days.

7. Pray Bold Prayers:

Confidence grows when you walk closely with God. He empowers you through the Holy Spirit to do things beyond your natural ability.

> "In Him and through faith in Him we may approach God with freedom and confidence."
>
> —Ephesians 3:12 (NIV)

- Action Step: Begin each day by asking God to lead you with boldness, clarity, and courage. Pray out loud—it reinforces belief.

Remember: Confidence isn't about being perfect or fearless—it's about being faithful and fully convinced that God is with you. As you take small steps of obedience, confidence will rise.

Scriptural Encouragement:

- Hebrews 10:35 – "So do not throw away your confidence; it will be richly rewarded."
- Joshua 1:9 – "Be strong and courageous. Do not be afraid; do not be discouraged, for the Lord your God will be with you wherever you go."
- Isaiah 41:10 – "Do not fear, for I am with you; do not be dismayed, for I am your God."

Self-Talk: Rewiring Confidence Through Words

Proverbs 18:21 reminds us: "The tongue has the power of life and death."

The way we speak to ourselves directly shapes our confidence. Our inner dialogue—whether positive or negative—influences our mindset and even rewires our brain through a process called neuroplasticity.

When we engage in negative self-talk, telling ourselves "I'm not good enough" or "I always mess up," our brain strengthens pathways that reinforce fear, doubt, and insecurity. Over time, these thoughts become automatic, shaping how we see ourselves, how we approach challenges, and whether we step into opportunities or shrink away from them.

But here's the good news—this can change. By intentionally shifting to positive self-talk, we create new neural pathways that foster confidence, resilience, and success. When we consistently affirm truths like "I am capable," "I can handle this," or "God has equipped me for this moment," our brain begins to accept and reinforce these beliefs, making confidence our default mindset.

Example: The Power of Words in Action

Imagine two people preparing for a big presentation. One says, "I'm going to mess this up. I'm terrible at public speaking." The other tells themselves: "I've prepared well. I have valuable insights to share. I can do this." Who do you think will walk in with greater confidence?

The second person has trained their brain to expect success, while the first has conditioned themselves for failure. The words we speak shape our reality—whether we step forward in boldness or hold ourselves back in fear.

How to Rewire Your Brain for Confidence:

- Catch Negative Thoughts – Pay attention to moments of self-doubt.
- Challenge the Lies – Ask yourself: Is this thought true, or is fear talking?
- Replace with Truth – Speak affirmations that align with God's promises and your strengths.
- Repeat Daily – The more you reinforce positive self-talk, the stronger those confidence-building pathways become.

Studies show that positive self-talk significantly improves self-confidence and mental well-being. Research highlights:
- Boosts Self-Perception – Reframes negative thoughts, leading to a stronger self-image.
- Reduces Stress & Anxiety – Optimistic inner dialogue promotes emotional stability.
- Enhances Performance – Athletes, professionals, and students who practice positive affirmations tend to perform better under pressure.
- Strengthens Mental Resilience – Encouraging self-talk fosters perseverance, helping individuals overcome setbacks.

Start Speaking Life Over Yourself:

Every day, declare:

- "I am equipped for success."
- "God has given me everything I need."
- "I can do all things through Christ."
- "I will succeed."

Confidence isn't just a feeling—it's a habit we create through the way we speak to ourselves. Choose words that build you up, and watch your confidence grow!

Preparation Builds Confidence:

One of the most valuable lessons I learned early in my business career was that preparation is the foundation of confidence. When I first started out, I was naturally shy, and each meeting with customers or executives felt overwhelming. Doubts clouded my mind—I worried about saying the wrong thing and questioned whether I was truly capable of meeting the expectations of my role.

Then, one day, a senior executive called me into his office. My heart sank—I was sure this was the moment my fears would come true, that I was about to be reprimanded. I tried to appear calm as I entered, but I knew my nervousness showed.

To my surprise, he welcomed me warmly. He smiled, joked, and engaged me in conversation. His office walls were decorated with pictures of airplanes, and he spoke passionately about his love for flying. He asked about my life, my goals, and my family. In just a few minutes, I felt at ease. He was a seasoned leader who understood how to build connections, control a room, and put others at ease.

Then he said something that stuck with me: "I was young once. Others helped me, and I want to help you." One of the greatest lessons he taught me was about preparation. He said, "Be prepared—preparation builds confidence. Be on time. Be yourself. Be positive." That simple advice changed the way I approached meetings, negotiations, and leadership opportunities.

Instead of walking into a room with fear and uncertainty, I began walking in prepared—and that preparation became the cornerstone of my confidence. To this day, before any meeting, whether it's a business discussion, pastoral counseling, or mentorship, I take time to outline the meeting, prepare my thoughts, and gather any necessary documentation.

- "Preparation lowers panic—when you're ready, you're steady.
- "Prepared people walk in peace; unprepared people walk on eggshells."

Failure: An Arch Enemy to Confidence

Many struggle with confidence because past failures haunt them. They remember the rejection, embarrassment, and mistakes, assuming that failure is permanent. But failure is not final—it's a lesson, a stepping stone toward success.

Some of the most successful people in history faced major setbacks before achieving greatness. Their stories prove that failure is not the end—it's part of the journey.

Famous People Who Overcame Failure:

- Abraham Lincoln – Lost multiple elections before becoming one of America's greatest presidents.
- Thomas Edison – Failed thousands of times before inventing the light bulb.
- Winston Churchill – Faced political failures and setbacks before leading Britain to victory in WWII.
- Oprah Winfrey – Fired from her first TV job for being "unfit for television" before becoming a media icon.
- Robert G. LeTourneau – Faced $100,000 in debt and nearly lost everything before building an industrial empire.

Biblical Figures Who Overcame Failure:

- Peter – Denied Jesus three times, but was later restored and became a foundational leader in the early church.
- David – Committed serious sins, including adultery and murder, yet repented and remained a man after God's own heart.

- Elijah – After experiencing great victories, he fell into deep despair, but God restored him and continued to use him.
- Paul – Persecuted Christians before encountering Jesus and becoming one of the most influential apostles.
- Moses – Killed an Egyptian in anger and fled into exile, yet God called him to lead Israel out of slavery.

The Psychology of Overcoming Failure:

Failure can trigger self-doubt, fear, and avoidance behaviors. Psychologists have found that people often associate failure with shame, leading them to hesitate before trying again. However, research shows that reframing failure as a learning opportunity can help individuals build resilience and move forward with confidence.

How to Rewire Your Mindset After Failure:

- Recognize Negative Thoughts – Acknowledge self-doubt without letting it define you.
- Reframe Failure as Growth – Instead of saying "I failed," say "I learned something valuable."
- Practice Self-Compassion – Treat yourself with kindness, just as you would encourage a friend.
- Set Realistic Goals – Break challenges into small, manageable steps to rebuild confidence.
- Surround Yourself with Encouragement – Seek mentors and friends who uplift and inspire you.

Believe in yourself, especially when no one else will – Sasquatch

Confidence Unlocks Doors:

When you believe in yourself, combined with faith in God, you begin to walk in boldness, strength, and authority. You stop waiting for permission and start pursuing your destiny.

Are you ready to step into your confidence?

Small Group Lesson: Keys to Confidence – Believing in Yourself

Theme Scripture:

"So do not throw away your confidence; it will be richly rewarded."

—Hebrews 10:35 (NIV)

Opening Question:

- When was a time in your life when you felt truly confident? What made the difference?

Main Point:

Confidence isn't about being fearless or flawless—it's about trusting God's purpose in you, preparing well, and choosing faith over fear.

Key Insights:

1. Confidence is Built, not Born:
   - You don't "find" confidence—you develop it through intentional action, spiritual alignment, and self-belief.
   - *"Let the weak say, 'I am strong.'"—Joel 3:10*
2. Preparation Builds Confidence:
   - "Preparation lowers panic—when you're ready, you're steady."

- Walking into any situation prepared reduces anxiety and boosts peace of mind.
3. Confidence Impacts Every Area:
    - It builds trust, attracts opportunity, inspires others, and improves communication.
    - In business and relationships, people are drawn to confident, grounded leaders.
4. Failure Doesn't Disqualify You:
    - God uses broken, imperfect people—like Moses, Peter, and David—to do extraordinary things.
    - Confidence is not the absence of mistakes, but the courage to rise again.

Discussion Questions:

1. What lies or limiting beliefs have you struggled with that impact your confidence?
2. What does confidence in Christ look like compared to worldly confidence?
3. What practical steps can you take this week to grow your self-confidence?
4. Share a time when preparation helped you feel more confident—what changed?

Action Step:

Choose one area where you lack confidence—whether it's speaking up, leading, or trying something new. This week:

- Prepare intentionally.
- Speak life over yourself.
- Pray bold prayers.
- Step into it with faith.

Prayer:

Father, thank You for the identity we have in You. Teach us to walk in boldness, not fear. Help us silence doubt, speak truth over our lives, and prepare well for the things You've called us to. Give us the courage to believe in ourselves the way You believe in us. In Jesus' name, Amen.

CHAPTER 6

THE COURAGE TO DO "THE HARD THING"

"Do what is easy and your life will be hard. Do what is hard and your life will be easy."

—LES BROWN

Every great victory, every life-changing decision, and every bold step toward fulfilling a dream requires courage. But courage is not the absence of fear—it's the choice to move forward despite fear. It is the mindset that refuses to remain stuck, the determination that pushes past uncertainty, and the unwavering belief that God has more in store for you. We must determine in our hearts to "do the hard thing."

Many people desire growth but hesitate when faced with challenges, risks, and the unknown. But here's the truth: Without courage, there is no advancement. Whether it's stepping into a new business venture, pursuing a calling, or making a decision that alters your future, it all comes down to this—do you have the courage to move forward?

John Wayne famously said, "Courage is being scared to death, but saddling up anyway."

Jeff Bezos and Amazon:

The story of Amazon's early days is a perfect example of taking a terrifying leap and risking everything. Jeff Bezos had a comfortable job on Wall Street when he decided to walk away from financial security to pursue his dream of building an online bookstore. At the time, e-commerce was still a new concept, and many people doubted its potential. But Bezos saw something others didn't—he believed the internet would revolutionize shopping.

Starting Amazon wasn't easy. He left his stable career, invested nearly all his savings, and convinced 22 investors to take a chance on his vision. Even then, success was far from guaranteed. In the early years, Amazon struggled financially, and Bezos had to fight to keep the company afloat. There were moments when it seemed like the business might collapse before it even took off. But he refused to quit. He pushed through rejection, setbacks, and uncertainty, believing that if he stayed the course, Amazon could become something extraordinary.

Today, Amazon is one of the most successful companies in the world, but it all started with one risky decision—leaving behind security to chase a dream. Bezos' story proves that stepping into the unknown, even when failure seems likely, can lead to something far greater than imagined.

Biblical Examples of Courage in Action:

The Bible is full of people who had to find courage to advance, even when the odds were against them. Many of these individuals were faced with "doing the hard thing." And they faced their fear and achieved much.

Joshua Leading Israel into the Promised Land (Joshua 1:9). After Moses died, Joshua was tasked with leading an entire nation into the unknown. The responsibility was overwhelming, but God told him, "Be strong and courageous. Do not be afraid; do not be discouraged, for the Lord your God will be with you wherever you go." Joshua chose courage, and it led Israel to victory.

Esther Risking Her Life to Save a Nation (Esther 4:14). Esther faced a choice—stay silent and watch her people perish, or step forward and risk her life before the king. She chose courage, saying, "If I perish, I perish." Because of her boldness, an entire nation was saved.

David Facing Goliath (1 Samuel 17:45-47). A young shepherd boy stepped onto a battlefield against a giant warrior. Human logic said he would lose, but courage—fueled by faith in God—gave him victory.

Peter Walking on Water (Matthew 14:29). When Peter saw Jesus walking on water, he had the courage to step out. Despite the storm, he moved forward. His courage brought him closer to Jesus in ways that fear never could.

Our Personal Journey of "Doing the Hard Thing"

My wife and I knew that God was calling us into full-time ministry, but I found myself torn between two passions—business and ministry. The business world provided stability, a reliable income, and a life I genuinely enjoyed. As VP of Sales and Marketing, I loved the corporate environment, managing products, marketing ventures, and customer relations. It was busy, demanding, but fulfilling.

Yet, I couldn't shake the growing sense of God's call. It weighed on me daily, pressing into my heart in a way I could not ignore. I knew the right thing—the hard thing—was to step out in faith. But this wasn't just any ministry opportunity—God was calling me to pastor my grandfather's church, a once-vibrant congregation now dwindled to about 35 people on a Sunday. No savings, no financial security, almost no cash flow. Truthfully, I had hoped God's call would lead us to a thriving, established church—something secure. But deep down, my wife and I knew this was His will.

I spent many sleepless nights wrestling with the decision, playing out scenarios in my mind. Was I crazy to walk away from financial security into a ministry with no stability? The logical choice was to stay in business. The right choice was following God's lead.

As I prayed, something shifted. God began to stir vision in my heart. Plans and ideas for the church started to form. Confidence grew as I outlined them, and with that confidence came peace.

Then the moment came—I sat in front of my computer, staring at my resignation letter. I prayed, took a deep breath, and submitted it. My company agreed to provide financial support for a few months to help with the transition, but beyond that, faith would carry us the rest of the way.

After resigning, I walked to my car. The sun had been baking the interior, making it hot and suffocating. I opened the armrest to grab my sunglasses, but instead, I saw three pennies lying alone inside. At that moment, God's voice spoke to me—clear, strong, loving:

"Do what I have called you to do, and you will never lack a penny." Tears welled in my eyes. It was God's reassurance—a promise that this journey was not mine alone. He was with me.

That was in 2007. We stepped out in faith and committed fully to the call. Over time, the church began to heal, grow, and thrive. We planted new works, expanded ministries, and found ourselves traveling to nations, training leaders, and ministering to people worldwide. God kept His word. We never missed a bill, never lacked provision. His faithfulness sustained us, even in uncertain seasons.

Looking back, I'm grateful that fear didn't rob us of God's dream for our lives. It wasn't easy—but faith requires stepping into the unknown, trusting that God will meet you there. You can do "the hard thing."

How to Cultivate Courage to Do "the Hard Thing"

If you're struggling with hesitation or fear, here are a few ways to build courage and move forward:

1. Identify Your Fears:

Courage isn't the absence of fear—it's the ability to act despite it. Start by recognizing what holds you back. Write down your fears and examine their root causes. Understanding them helps you take control rather than letting them control you.

Another practice is to separate the emotion. Try looking at the situation without the lens of fear. By separating the fear, we can weigh things out and come to a logical answer.

2. Reframe Your Mindset:

Fear often stems from negative thinking. Instead of seeing challenges as threats, view them as opportunities for growth. Shift your perspective from *"What if I fail?"* to *"What if I succeed?"* This simple change can make a huge difference in how you approach difficult situations.

> *"In any moment of decision, the best thing you can do is the right thing, the next best thing is the wrong thing, and the worst thing you can do is nothing."*
>
> — Theodore Roosevelt

3. Take Small, Consistent Steps:

Courage grows through action. Start with small steps outside your comfort zone. Whether it's speaking up in a meeting, trying something new, or facing a difficult conversation, each step builds confidence and resilience.

4. Prepare and Plan:

Uncertainty fuels fear. The more prepared you are, the more confident you'll feel. Research, practice, and strategize before taking action. Whether it's a big decision or a personal challenge, preparation reduces anxiety and strengthens courage.

5. Embrace Failure as a Teacher:

Fear of failure can paralyze you. Instead of avoiding mistakes, learn from them. Every setback is an opportunity to grow, adjust, and improve. The most successful people have failed many times—but they kept going.

Bonus Step: Surround Yourself with Encouragement

Courage thrives in the right environment. Seek mentors, friends, or role models who inspire and challenge you. Their support can help you push past fear and step into bold action.

Courage Changes Everything:

The choice to move forward—despite uncertainty, fear, and setbacks—will determine how far you go in life. Do you have the courage to advance? Your destiny is waiting. Your breakthrough is ahead. And God is with you.

Small Group Discussion – Chapter 6: *The Courage To Do "The Hard Thing"*

Key Quote:

"Do what is easy and your life will be hard. Do what is hard and your life will be easy."

— Les Brown

Opening Reflection:

What's one "hard thing" you've faced recently? Did you avoid it, confront it, or are you still in the middle of it?

Discussion Questions:

1. What does "doing the hard thing" look like in your life right now?
   Is there a decision or step of faith you've been putting off?
2. Think of Joshua, Esther, or David.
   What gave them the courage to move forward—and how can that apply to you?
3. What fear or excuse is most likely to keep you from moving forward?
   How can you reframe that fear with faith?
4. The author shared a powerful moment of surrender.
   Have you ever had a defining moment where God asked you to trust Him with everything? What happened?

5. What practical step can you take this week to build courage? (Small action, conversation, prayer, or plan?)

Scriptures for Strength:

- *Joshua 1:9* – "Be strong and courageous . . . the Lord your God will be with you wherever you go."
- *Esther 4:14* – "Perhaps you were born for such a time as this."
- *2 Timothy 1:7* – "God has not given us a spirit of fear..."

Action Step:

Identify one "hard thing" you need to face. Write it down.

Then, list one small step you can take this week toward it. Pray and ask God for the courage to act.

Prayer Focus:

Ask God to replace fear with faith, to speak clearly into areas of decision, and to give supernatural courage for every member of your group.

Courage isn't loud—it's the quiet decision to obey, even when it's hard.

CHAPTER 7

MENTORS – THE GREAT SHORTCUT

"A mentor is someone who sees more talent and ability within you than you see in yourself, and helps bring it out of you."

—Bob Proctor

"A lot of people have gone further than they thought they could because someone else thought they could."

—Zig Ziglar

Success is rarely a solo journey. Behind every great leader, entrepreneur, and athlete, there is often a mentor—someone who has walked the path before and offers wisdom, guidance, and encouragement. Mentors are the great shortcut to success, helping us avoid unnecessary mistakes, refine our vision, and pursue our dreams with excellence.

Many people struggle because they try to figure everything out on their own. This is pride. Pride will hold you back. But God designed life to be relational, and mentorship is one of the most powerful ways to accelerate growth. Whether in business, ministry, or personal development, the right mentor can change everything.

Biblical Examples of Mentorship:

The Bible is filled with mentor-mentee relationships that shaped history. Here are some of the most powerful examples:

1. Moses and Joshua - Moses mentored Joshua, preparing him to lead Israel into the Promised Land. Joshua learned leadership, faith, and strategy from Moses, and when the time came, he stepped into his calling with confidence.
2. Elijah and Elisha - Elijah trained Elisha in prophetic ministry, passing down wisdom and anointing. Because of this mentorship, Elisha performed twice as many miracles as Elijah.
3. Paul and Timothy - Paul mentored Timothy, teaching him how to lead churches, preach the Gospel, and stay strong in faith. Paul's letters to Timothy are filled with encouragement and instruction, showing the power of mentorship.
4. Jethro and Moses - Jethro, Moses' father-in-law, taught Moses how to delegate leadership. Without Jethro's wisdom, Moses would have burned out trying to lead alone.
5. Jesus and His Disciples - Jesus was the ultimate mentor, training His disciples for ministry. He taught them how to pray, how to lead, and how to walk in faith, preparing them to spread the Gospel worldwide.

Business Leaders Who Had Mentors:

Many of the world's most successful entrepreneurs had mentors who guided them through challenges and helped them refine their vision.

1. Steve Jobs and Mark Zuckerberg - Steve Jobs mentored Mark Zuckerberg, helping him navigate the early days of Facebook. Their conversations shaped Zuckerberg's leadership and vision.
2. Warren Buffett and Bill Gates - Warren Buffett mentored Bill Gates, teaching him long-term thinking, investment strategies, and leadership principles.
3. Howard Schultz and Starbucks Mentors - Schultz, the former CEO of Starbucks, credits mentors in business and leadership for helping him build Starbucks into a global brand.
4. Oprah Winfrey and Maya Angelou - Oprah was mentored by Maya Angelou, who helped her navigate success, leadership, and personal growth.
5. Phil Knight and Bill Bowerman - The founder of Nike, Phil Knight, was mentored by his track coach, Bill Bowerman, who helped him develop the vision for Nike.

Athletes Who Had Mentors:

Athletes don't succeed alone—they rely on coaches, mentors, and advisors to sharpen their skills and mindset. The unteachable and prideful sit on the bench and miss great opportunities to be developed.

1. Tom Brady and Tom Martinez - Tom Brady credits his longtime mentor, Tom Martinez, for helping him refine his throwing mechanics and leadership skills.
2. Steph Curry and His Father, Dell Curry - Steph Curry was mentored by his father, Dell Curry, who taught him the fundamentals of basketball and leadership.
3. Mike Trout and Baseball Mentors - Mike Trout had mentors throughout his baseball career, helping him develop into one of the greatest players of his generation.
4. Joel Ward and His Big Brother Mentor - NHL player Joel Ward was a mentor himself, but he also had mentors who helped him navigate his career.
5. Patrice Bergeron and Leadership Mentors - Bergeron, a star in the NHL, was mentored by coaches and veteran players, shaping him in his exceptional leadership skills on and off the ice. One of his most significant mentors was Zdeno Chara, the longtime captain of the Boston Bruins.

The Power of Mentorship in Your Life:

Success is rarely a solo journey. Along the way, we need guides, encouragers, and wisdom-bearers—people who have walked ahead and can light the path forward. A mentor is more than just an advisor; they are a catalyst for growth, helping you navigate challenges and seize opportunities that might otherwise remain out of reach.

Here are some advantages:

- Wisdom from experience – Learning from a mentor's mistakes can save you years of trial and error. Their insights help you sidestep common pitfalls and approach decisions with greater clarity. They have already faced setbacks, learned hard lessons, and can now help you avoid unnecessary struggles.

- Encouragement in tough times – When discouragement sets in, a mentor reminds you why you started. They offer perspective when doubts creep in and serve as a steady voice, urging you not to quit when obstacles feel overwhelming. Sometimes, all you need is someone who believes in you when you struggle to believe in yourself.
- Accountability – Success isn't just about talent—it's about discipline and consistency. A mentor challenges you to stay focused, refine your skills, and push beyond your comfort zone. They hold you to a higher standard, ensuring you don't settle for less than your potential.
- Connections – The right mentor can open doors you never knew existed. Whether it's introductions to influential people, access to resources, or exposure to new opportunities, a mentor's network becomes an extension of your own success. What would take years to build alone can be accelerated through the right relationships. Mentorship is the difference between wandering aimlessly and walking with purpose. It's the fast track to growth, wisdom, and breakthrough, and it all starts with a willingness to learn.

Quotes:

"Nobody makes it alone. Nobody has made it alone."

— OPRAH WINFREY

"Show me a successful individual, and I'll show you someone who had real positive influences in his or her life. I don't care what you do for a living—if you do it well, I'm sure there was someone cheering you on or showing the way. A mentor."

—Denzel Washington

How to be Mentored:

Being mentored is more than just receiving advice—it's a relationship that refines, strengthens, and positions you for the future. A mentor provides wisdom, accountability, and encouragement, helping you avoid unnecessary mistakes and guiding you through challenges.

But mentorship is not passive—it requires intentional effort and humility from the one being mentored. It's not simply about having access to someone wise; it's about applying their guidance with diligence and commitment. A great mentor can open doors that you couldn't reach alone, but your willingness to listen, learn, and act determines how far you'll go.

In this section, we explore how to find the right mentor, how to cultivate a teachable spirit, and how to nurture a meaningful and lasting mentorship relationship. Learning to steward mentorship well can lead to transformation—not just in your career or personal growth, but in your faith, leadership, and ability to mentor others in the future.

1. Finding the Right Mentor: If you want to birth your dreams and do it with excellence, find a mentor who:
   - Has experience in your field.
   - Shares your values and vision.

- Challenges you to grow.
- Is willing to invest in your success.

2. Be Teachable & Humble:

   Mentorship isn't about showcasing what you already know—it's about embracing the opportunity to grow. A humble, teachable attitude is the key to unlocking wisdom. Nothing discourages a mentor more than someone unwilling to listen or consider new perspectives. On the other hand, few things are more rewarding than guiding someone who genuinely values insight and applies it with intentionality.

   Being teachable means approaching mentorship with curiosity, openness, and a willingness to learn, knowing that growth comes not from proving yourself, but from refining your understanding.

- Listen more than you speak – Take in their insights fully before responding. Honor their experience by giving space for their wisdom to shape your perspective.
- Take notes – Show that you value their guidance by writing down key points and reflections. Thoughtful note-taking not only helps retention but also demonstrates respect for their time and expertise.
- Apply feedback – Growth isn't just about hearing advice; it's about implementing it. When a mentor sees you applying what they've shared, they'll invest in you even more.
- Ask insightful questions – Curiosity is a sign of humility. Thoughtful questions show that you are eager to learn, not just to receive answers, but to understand deeper truths.

- Stay open to correction – Refinement requires adjustment. A mentor's correction isn't criticism—it's a gift that helps shape you for greater success.

Proverbs 1:5 – "Let the wise hear and increase in learning, and the one who understands obtain guidance."

4. Respect the Mentor's Time & Wisdom - A mentor's time is valuable, so approach them with intentionality and preparation.

    How to honor a mentor:
    - Be prepared – Come with specific questions and topics.
    - Respect their schedule – Don't expect unlimited time; make meetings count.
    - Follow through – If they give advice, implement it. Show commitment.
    - Express gratitude – A simple "thank you" shows appreciation.

Hebrews 13:7 – "Remember your leaders, who spoke the word of God to you. Consider the outcome of their way of life and imitate their faith."

5. Build a Relationship, Not Just a Transaction. Mentorship should be mutual and meaningful. A mentor is not just a source of answers—they are a guide in life.
    - Learn about your mentor's journey – Understand their challenges and victories.
    - Offer value – If possible, find ways to encourage or assist them in projects.
    - Keep in touch – Don't only reach out when you need advice. Build a lasting relationship.

- Don't wear them out – Understand that their time is valuable.

Example: Joshua learned directly from Moses by staying close to him, watching his leadership, and absorbing wisdom (Exodus 33:11).

6. Apply & Share What You Learn. True growth happens when you put wisdom into action. Don't just take notes—live out what you learn.
   - Implement advice – Take action on what your mentor teaches you.
   - Pass it on – Share wisdom with others; become a mentor to someone else.
   - Stay accountable – Keep your mentor updated on how their guidance has helped.

2 Timothy 2:2 – "And the things you have heard me say in the presence of many witnesses, entrust to reliable people who will also be qualified to teach others."

Your Shortcut to Success:

Mentorship is not just advice—it's a shortcut to excellence. The right mentor can change your life, refine your vision, and help you step into your calling with confidence.

Small Group Discussion – Chapter 7: *Mentors – The Great Shortcut*

Key Quote:

"A mentor is someone who sees more talent and ability within you than you see in yourself, and helps bring it out of you."

—Bob Proctor

Opening Icebreaker:

Share about someone who's made a positive impact in your life—a teacher, coach, leader, or friend. What did they do that helped you grow?

Discussion Questions:

1. Why do you think so many people try to figure things out alone instead of seeking mentorship?
   Have you ever tried to do something without help and later realized you needed guidance?
2. Look at the biblical examples (Moses & Joshua, Elijah & Elisha, Paul & Timothy).
   Which of these relationships stands out to you, and why?
3. What qualities make someone a good mentor?
   What qualities make someone a good *mentee*?
4. Do you currently have someone in your life who mentors you (formally or informally)?
   If not, what's one step you can take to seek out mentorship?
5. Mentorship is a shortcut—but it requires humility.

Which point in the "How to Be Mentored" section challenged you the most? Why?

Scripture Focus:

- *Proverbs 1:5* – "Let the wise hear and increase in learning, and the one who understands obtain guidance."
- *Hebrews 13:7* – "Remember your leaders . . . imitate their faith."
- *2 Timothy 2:2* – Pass on what you've learned to others.

Action Step:

Take time this week to:

1. Identify one potential mentor in your life—someone you respect and can learn from.
2. Write down one way you can approach them intentionally and humbly.
3. Pray for a teachable spirit and divine connections.

Group Prayer Focus:

Ask God to give each person the humility to be mentored and the wisdom to pursue the right relationships. Pray for divine alignment with mentors who will call out purpose and destiny.

Mentorship is a bridge to your future. Walk it with honor, humility, and intentionality.

CHAPTER 8

BREAKING BAD HABITS – CREATING GOOD HABITS

"Your habits will determine your future."

—Jack Canfield

Success isn't just about talent, opportunity, or luck—it's about habits. The small, daily choices we make shape our future. Good habits propel us forward, while bad habits hold us back. If we're not intentional, unhealthy patterns can kill or delay our dreams, keeping us stuck in cycles of frustration.

The enemy's greatest deception is convincing you that destructive habits won't affect your outcome—that you can make poor choices and still expect success. But habits shape your future—what you repeat in private eventually manifests in your life. If you cultivate discipline and wisdom, you'll reap strength and victory, but if you allow compromise and neglect, you'll face struggles and setbacks. True transformation begins with the habits we choose daily.

An Unorganized Engineer: Learning the Hard Way

Years ago, our company hired a brilliant young electronics engineer named Jim. His talent was undeniable—he was sharp, creative, and had a deep understanding of his field. From the moment he joined the team, it was clear that he had something special. As I tested him with smaller projects and later entrusted him with more significant tasks, I was continually impressed. Some people seem to have an innate gifting, and Jim was one of them.

However, after about four months, I began to notice serious issues—bad habits that started to overshadow his brilliance. Despite his technical genius, his poor personal hygiene, office clutter, and chronic lateness became increasingly problematic. I couldn't understand it. How could someone so gifted be so careless with fundamental professional expectations?

One day, I had an important meeting with IBM regarding a high-quality, low-cost printer project. I asked Jim to attend, expecting him to represent our team well, field questions, and take notes. The meeting was scheduled to begin at 8:00 AM sharp—a crucial time when first impressions mattered. But when the executives arrived, Jim strolled in ten minutes late, looking completely unprepared. His hair was unkempt, his shirt looked slept in, and his overall appearance sent the wrong message. I could see the puzzled expressions on the executives' faces. In that moment, I knew they were silently questioning the credibility of our company.

After the meeting, I knew a serious conversation was needed. I praised his talent, but I also addressed the undeniable issue—his poor habits were becoming a liability. He dismissed them as minor, unaware of how much they were holding him back. So I had to be direct: If these habits didn't change, he wouldn't be able to stay. The realization shook him. For the first time, he understood the weight of his actions.

To his credit, Jim took the conversation seriously. Just days later, I noticed a significant shift—his workspace was clean, he was well-groomed, and he had taken steps to improve his professionalism. Over time, I trusted him again with high-level projects, and he thrived. His brilliance was never the issue; it was his discipline and awareness that needed sharpening.

Addressing these bad habits wasn't easy, but it helped shape him into a highly successful engineer, proving that talent alone isn't enough—personal discipline and professional awareness are just as essential.

Samson: Wasted Potential and the Power of Redemption:

Samson was born with extraordinary potential. From the moment of his birth, he was set apart as a Nazirite, chosen by God to deliver Israel from the Philistines. He possessed unmatched physical strength, a gift that made him one of the most powerful figures in the Old Testament.

But despite his divine calling, Samson's bad habits and poor choices led him down a path of self-destruction. Instead of using his strength for God's purposes, Samson often acted impulsively, driven by personal desires rather than wisdom. He ignored his Nazirite vows, pursued immoral relationships that weakened him, and allowed pride and recklessness to dictate his actions. His obsession with Delilah ultimately led to his downfall—he revealed the secret of his strength, was betrayed, and ended up blind and enslaved by the very enemies he was meant to defeat.

His story is a powerful warning—talent and calling alone are not enough. Without self-control and wisdom, even the most gifted individuals can fall short of their destiny.

Samson's story takes a turn toward redemption. Broken, blind, and humbled, he cried out to God one last time. In an act of faith and repentance, he destroyed the Philistine temple, defeating Israel's enemies and fulfilling his purpose—though not in the way he could have if he had walked in obedience from the start.

Samson's life teaches us that bad habits can rob us of our potential, but God's grace is always available. No matter how many mistakes we've made, it's never too late to turn back, seek God, and step into His purpose.

Breaking Bad Habits Before They Break You:

Samson's downfall wasn't one bad decision—it was a series of small compromises that led to his destruction. His story reminds us that:

- Unchecked habits can derail even the most gifted individuals.
- Discipline and obedience matter more than raw talent.
- God's grace is always available, even after failure.

If Samson had recognized his weaknesses earlier, he could have led Israel into a golden age of victory. But his lack of self-control cost him everything.

The Power of Healthy Habits: "A Life Transformed."

I created this story for impact. After researching this topic, I decided to use multiple examples to create one story that illustrates the power of healthy habits. Let's call her Sarah. She is a busy professional who once struggled with stress, fatigue, and unhealthy habits. Her demanding job left her exhausted, and she often relied on fast food, late nights, and little exercise to get through the day. Over time, she felt burned out, disconnected, overweight, and stuck in a cycle of frustration.

One day, Sarah decided she had to make a change. She started small—waking up earlier, prioritizing prayer and reflection, and making healthier food choices. She committed to daily exercise, even if it was just a short walk. She replaced negative self-talk with affirmations of faith and strength.

At first, the changes felt insignificant, but over time, they transformed her life. She gained energy, clarity, and confidence. Her relationships improved, her work performance soared, she began to look healthy, and she felt closer to God than ever before.

Sarah's journey proves that small, consistent habits lead to lasting transformation. She didn't just change her routine—she changed her mindset, and that shift opened doors to blessings she never imagined.

The Lesson? Healthy Habits Unlock a Blessed Life:

- Faith and discipline create momentum.
- Small steps lead to big breakthroughs.
- Your daily choices shape your future.

Sarah's story is a reminder that change is possible—and when you commit to healthy habits, you set yourself up for a life of strength, joy, and purpose.

What Are Habits?

Habits are automatic behaviors—things we do without thinking. They are formed through repetition, and over time, they become ingrained in our daily lives. Some habits build success, while others create roadblocks.

- Good habits lead to growth, discipline, and achievement.
- Bad habits lead to stagnation, frustration, and failure.

The Psychology of Habits - Why We Form Them & How to Change Them:

Habits form due to a cue-routine-reward cycle:

- Cue – A trigger that starts the behavior.
- Routine – The habit itself.
- Reward – The satisfaction or result that reinforces the habit.

Breaking a bad habit takes consistent effort over time. Studies show that 21 days is the minimum, but true transformation can take up to 66 days of repeated action. During the process of habit formation, the brain creates neural pathways that make habits feel automatic. If the habit provides emotional relief, quitting feels uncomfortable. Change requires intentional effort and replacing old patterns.

Where Do Bad Habits Come From?

Bad habits don't appear overnight—they develop over time. They often stem from:

- Comfort zones – Choosing what's easy instead of what's best.
- Fear – Avoiding challenges because of self-doubt.
- Influence – Picking up unhealthy behaviors from others.
- Lack of discipline – Failing to set boundaries or healthy routines.

The Cost of Bad Habits:

Bad habits steal time, energy, and opportunity. They can:

- Delay success – Procrastination keeps dreams on hold.
- Damage relationships – Poor communication or negativity pushes people away.
- Hurt our health – Unhealthy eating, lack of exercise, or stress can take a toll.
- Weaken faith – Neglecting prayer, Scripture, or spiritual growth leads to distance from God.

Breaking Bad Habits:

Breaking bad habits is possible but requires intentional effort. Here's how:

- Identify the Habit – Be honest about what's holding you back.
- Understand the Root Cause – Where did it come from? Why do you keep doing it?
- Replace it with a Good Habit – Don't just stop—start something better.

- Create Accountability – Surround yourself with people who challenge you to grow.
- Stay Consistent – Change takes time. Keep going, even when it's hard.

Creating Good Habits for Success:

If you want to excel in ministry, business, or family, develop habits that promote growth:

- Start your day with prayer and reflection – Strengthen your faith.
- Set clear goals – Know where you're going.
- Practice discipline – Stick to routines that build success.
- Invest in relationships – Surround yourself with positive influences.
- Keep learning – Read, study, and grow in wisdom.
- We don't do things because they are easy; we do them because they are right.

Quotes on Habits:

- "We are what we repeatedly do. Excellence, then, is not an act, but a habit."—Will Durant
- "The chains of habit are too weak to be felt until they are too strong to be broken."—Samuel Johnson
- "Motivation is what gets you started. Habit is what keeps you going."—Jim Ryun

Real-World Examples of Habit Change:

Many successful people had to break bad habits to move forward:
- Charles Duhigg – Author of *The Power of Habit*, he struggled with unhealthy routines until he learned how to retrain his brain.
- Dave Ramsey – Before becoming a financial expert, he had poor money habits that led to bankruptcy. He changed his approach and built a thriving business.
- John Maxwell – Early in his leadership journey, he had to develop habits of discipline and consistency to become an influential speaker and author.

Ministers Who Overcame Bad Habits:

Even spiritual leaders have struggled with habits that held them back:

- Billy Graham – Early in his ministry, he had to break the habit of overcommitting, learning to balance his time wisely.
- Charles Spurgeon – He battled self-doubt and discouragement, but developed habits of prayer and study to strengthen his faith. He also struggled with smoking cigars. He loved this bad habit, but it was greatly affecting his ministry. He ultimately faced the fact that it was making believers stumble, and God gave him the grace to quit.
- John Wesley – He had to overcome unhealthy leadership habits, learning to delegate and trust others.

Common Bad Habits Among Small Business Owners:

Running a small business comes with challenges, and certain habits can unintentionally slow progress or limit success. Here are some common pitfalls that business owners often face:

- Micromanaging – Struggling to delegate tasks, leading to burnout and inefficiency.
- Poor financial management – Ignoring budgets, overspending, or failing to track cash flow properly.
- Neglecting marketing – Relying on word-of-mouth alone instead of actively promoting the business.
- Avoiding difficult decisions – Delaying necessary changes due to fear or uncertainty.
- Failing to adapt – Sticking to outdated methods instead of evolving with industry trends.
- Overworking – Not setting boundaries, leading to exhaustion and decreased productivity.
- Ignoring customer feedback – Dismissing complaints or failing to improve based on client input.
- Lack of employee development – Not investing in training or creating a positive work culture.

Common Bad Habits Among Ministry Leaders:

Leading in ministry comes with great responsibility, but certain habits can hinder effectiveness and spiritual impact. Here are some common pitfalls ministry leaders should be mindful of:

- Neglecting personal spiritual growth – Pouring into others while failing to nurture their own relationship with God.
- Micromanaging – Struggling to delegate, leading to burnout and limiting team development.
- Avoiding difficult conversations – Hesitating to address conflict or necessary changes, allowing issues to fester.
- Overcommitting – Saying "yes" to everything, leading to exhaustion and diminished effectiveness.
- Failing to equip others – Doing everything themselves instead of empowering others to lead.
- Ignoring self-care – Neglecting rest, family, and personal well-being in the name of ministry.
- Resisting change – Holding onto outdated methods instead of adapting to new opportunities for growth.
- Lack of accountability – Leading without seeking wise counsel or allowing others to speak into their life.
- Focusing too much on numbers – Measuring success solely by attendance or finances rather than spiritual transformation.
- Neglecting mentorship – Failing to invest in the next generation of leaders, leaving a gap in leadership development.
- Neglecting future vision – Leading only for today without planning for sustainability, long-term impact, or the next season of ministry.

Recognizing and addressing these habits can lead to stronger leadership, healthier ministry, and a deeper impact on those being served.

Your Habits Shape Your Future:

If you want to achieve your dreams, take an honest look at your habits. What's helping you? What's holding you back? The good news is—you can change. With faith, discipline, and intentional effort, you can build habits that lead to great success.

Small Group Discussion – Chapter 8: *Breaking Bad Habits – Creating Good Habits*

Key Quote:

"Your habits will determine your future."

—Jack Canfield

Icebreaker:

Name one habit—good or bad—that shaped your last year. What impact did it have?

Discussion Questions:

1. Why do small habits have such a big impact over time?
   Think about Sarah's story—what habits transformed her life?
2. Samson had talent but lacked discipline.
   Why isn't talent alone enough for success? What habits caused his downfall?
3. Which bad habit have you struggled with that's delayed your progress?
   What's one small step you could take to break it?
4. What does it mean to "replace a bad habit with a good one"?
   Why is this more effective than just trying to "stop" something?

5. Which good habit would make the biggest difference in your spiritual life, business, or leadership?

Scripture Focus:

- *Proverbs 25:28* – "A man without self-control is like a city broken into and left without walls."
- *Galatians 6:9* – "Let us not grow weary of doing good, for in due season we will reap, if we do not give up."
- *2 Timothy 1:7* – "For God gave us a spirit not of fear but of power and love and self-control."

Action Step:

1. Identify one bad habit you want to break.
2. Choose one good habit to replace it.
3. Share your commitment with the group for accountability.

Group Prayer Focus:

Pray for strength to break destructive patterns and for grace to build life-giving habits. Ask God for wisdom, discipline, and consistency to walk in His best.

Habits don't just form a routine—they form a future. Let's choose wisely.

CHAPTER 9

KILLING PROCRASTINATION

"You may delay, but time will not."
—BENJAMIN FRANKLIN

Procrastination is one of the most dangerous enemies to success. It's invisible, deceptive, and often disguised as a harmless delay. But make no mistake—procrastination kills dreams. It's as big of an enemy as Goliath was to David, standing in the way of progress, growth, and achievement.

Many people want to move forward with big dreams, but they keep putting things off. They say, "I'll start tomorrow," "I'll do it when I feel ready," or "I'll wait for the perfect time." But tomorrow never comes, and the perfect time never arrives.

Why Procrastination Happens:

Procrastination isn't just laziness—it's often rooted in deeper issues. Procrastination is largely influenced by dopamine, the brain's reward neurotransmitter. Dopamine plays a critical role in motivation, pleasure, and decision-making, often driving us toward instant gratification rather than long-term productivity. It can also be based in other areas as listed below:

- Fear of failure – People delay action because they're afraid of making mistakes.
- Perfectionism – Some wait until everything is perfect before starting, which leads to endless delays.
- Lack of motivation – Without a clear vision, it's easy to push things aside.
- Distractions – Social media, entertainment, and busyness keep people from focusing on what truly matters.
- Overwhelm – When a task feels too big, people avoid it instead of breaking it into smaller steps.
- Reward – People create bad productivity habits based on doing things that make them feel a sense of instant reward.

Real-Life Stories of Overcoming Procrastination:

Kieran Behan – He was a gymnast who refused to quit. He was told he would never walk again after a failed surgery at the age of ten. He could have given up, he could have put things off, always waiting until he felt up to things, but instead, he fought through pain, setbacks, and discouragement. He spent 15 months in a wheelchair, then suffered a severe head injury that set him back even further. But he refused to procrastinate on his dream. He kept training, kept pushing forward, and eventually became an Olympic gymnast.

Rev. Chad Brooks – Overcoming ministry procrastination. Rev. Chad Brooks struggled with serial procrastination for years.

He realized that procrastination wasn't just about motivation—it was about energy and focus. As a pastoral coach, he learned to identify the root causes of procrastination and developed strategies to defeat it. Today, he helps others break free from procrastination and step into productive ministry.

A humorous classic Irish twist on procrastination is:
"Never do today what you can put off until tomorrow."
Or, for an even worse version:
"Why do today what you can put off until next year?"
The Irish certainly have a way of making even procrastination sound charming!

How to Defeat Procrastination:

When David went into battle against Goliath, he had a battle plan. He chose five smooth stones that could fit into his sling. He chose not to wear the heavy armor, and he also chose to run quickly toward this fearful enemy. We know the story, but the point is, he had the right plan. He defeated an enemy that paralyzed Israel with fear. Procrastination paralyzed Israel's progress. If you want to kill procrastination, you need a battle plan:

Defeating Procrastination: Action Steps

1. Take Immediate Action – Stop waiting for the perfect time—it doesn't exist. The longer you delay, the harder it becomes to start. Even if it's just a small step, take action now. Momentum builds when you move, not when you overthink.

2. Break Tasks into Small Steps – Feeling overwhelmed often leads to delay. Instead of viewing the entire task as a mountain, focus on one manageable step at a time. Small victories add up, and before you know it, the task is complete.
3. Set Deadlines – Without deadlines, tasks tend to linger indefinitely. Give yourself realistic but firm deadlines, and hold yourself accountable. A set timeline creates urgency, making it harder to push things off.
4. Eliminate Distractions – Distractions sabotage productivity. Create a focused environment by turning off notifications, setting boundaries, and prioritizing what truly matters. Your surroundings shape your ability to concentrate—design them for success.
5. Develop a Routine – Success isn't built on motivation alone—it's built on consistent habits. Establish a daily rhythm that ensures progress, even on days when you don't feel like working. Structure breeds discipline. Structure brings progress!
6. Find Accountability – Surround yourself with people who push you forward, not enable procrastination. A mentor, coach, or even a friend can help keep you committed. Verbalizing your goals to others increases follow-through.

Each of these steps transforms procrastination into action, progress, and momentum. Small changes lead to big results.

Your Time is Now:

Procrastination is a thief—it steals time, opportunity, and success. But you don't have to let it win. You have the power to defeat it, step forward, and take action today. You have the power to be productive.

Are you ready to kill your "Goliath" of procrastination and move toward your destiny?

Small Group Lesson – Chapter 9: Killing Procrastination

Key Quote:

"You may delay, but time will not."
—Benjamin Franklin

Lesson Focus:

Procrastination is a hidden enemy that delays purpose, progress, and productivity. Like David's Goliath, it must be faced head-on. We don't wait for the perfect moment—we take action now.

Opening Question:

What's something you've been putting off? Why do you think you haven't started?

Read Together:

1 Samuel 17:45-48 – David ran quickly toward Goliath.

Proverbs 13:4 – "The soul of the sluggard craves and gets nothing, while the soul of the diligent is richly supplied."

Key Points to Discuss:

1. Why Do We Procrastinate?

Fear, perfectionism, overwhelm, distraction, or just habit? Which one do you struggle with most?

2. What Does Procrastination Steal?

   Missed opportunities, spiritual growth, business success, or relational health?

3. What's Your Goliath?

   Identify one big goal you've delayed—what's one small step you could take today?

Group Activity:

"Choose Your Stones"

– DAVID'S BATTLE PLAN

Write down five "stones" (action steps) you will use to defeat your procrastination this week. Share one with the group and commit to doing it in the next 48 hours.

Action Steps:

- ✓ Take Immediate Action
- ✓ Break It Down
- ✓ Set a Deadline
- ✓ Eliminate Distractions
- ✓ Create Structure
- ✓ Find Accountability

Closing Challenge:

"Don't let your destiny wait on your delay. The time to act is now."

_____

Group Prayer Focus:

Pray for courage to face the giant of procrastination. Ask for clarity, discipline, and momentum to act in obedience and faith.

CHAPTER 10

FREEDOM FROM LIMITING BELIEFS

"The battlefield of success and faith
is not in the wallet or the world,
but in the mind and heart."

—Bob Pittman

Everyone has a dream, a vision for something greater. But before many ever take their first step, they find themselves held back—not by circumstances, but by the beliefs they carry. These limiting beliefs are like invisible chains, keeping people stuck in a mindset that whispers, "You're not good enough," "This will never work," or "People like you don't succeed."

But here's the truth: What you believe shapes your reality. The wrong beliefs will shrink your future, but faith-filled, empowering beliefs will open doors to possibilities you never imagined.

Embrace discomfort.

Limiting beliefs don't vanish instantly—they take time to unlearn. Even when we recognize they're holding us back, shifting our mindset can feel like an uphill battle.

Science reveals that our brains reward us for clinging to familiar beliefs, reinforcing what we've accepted as truth. Breaking free from these mental patterns demands stepping into uncomfortable spaces—but discomfort is where growth begins.

Walt Disney:

A great example of overcoming limiting beliefs is Walt Disney. Early in his career, Disney faced repeated failures. He was fired from a newspaper job because his editor believed he "lacked creativity." His first animation company went bankrupt, and he struggled to find investors who believed in his vision. At times, he doubted whether he had what it took to succeed.

But instead of accepting defeat, Disney challenged his limiting beliefs. He refused to believe that failure defined him. He kept pushing forward, refining his ideas, and eventually created Mickey Mouse, which launched his empire.

His story proves that breaking free from limiting beliefs isn't about avoiding setbacks—it's about believing in your vision and taking action despite uncertainty.

Joyce Meyers:

Joyce Meyer's journey is a powerful example of overcoming limiting beliefs. Joyce grew up in a difficult environment, facing abuse and rejection from her father. These experiences planted deep-seated fears and insecurities, leading her to believe she was unworthy of love and success. Even as she stepped into ministry, she struggled with self-doubt, questioning whether she was truly capable of making an impact.

However, Joyce refused to let her past define her future. She began to reprogram her mind, replacing negative thoughts with biblical truths. She embraced God's promises, learning to see herself through His eyes rather than through the lens of past pain. Over time, she broke free from the fear of rejection and stepped boldly into her calling.

Today, Joyce Meyer is a globally recognized minister, author, and speaker, helping millions overcome their own limiting beliefs. Her story is a testament to the power of faith, mindset shifts, and perseverance in breaking free from emotional barriers.

The Lies That Hold Us Back:

Many people stay small because they believe lies about themselves—lies shaped by past failures, negative words, or fear. Below are a few common lies:

1. "I'm not talented enough."
   - This lie paralyzes creativity and confidence. Yet every major leader, athlete, or entrepreneur started somewhere—often with nothing but persistence and faith.
   - Consider Walt Disney, who was fired from a newspaper for "lacking imagination." If he had believed that label, he never would have built the entertainment empire that impacts the world today.

2. "I don't have the right connections."
   - People believe success is reserved for those who are born into privilege. But God opens doors no one can shut (Revelation 3:8).
   - Howard Schultz, the former CEO of Starbucks, grew up in a working-class family. He didn't come from wealth or elite connections, yet he built one of the most recognized brands on earth.
3. "I've failed too many times."
   - Failure is not the end—it's part of the journey. Thomas Edison failed over 1,000 times before he successfully invented the light bulb. Had he believed failure was permanent, the world would still be in the dark.
4. "I don't have enough resources."
   - While resources can help, they are not the deciding factor in success. Many people have built businesses, careers, and dreams with limited money, connections, or education. Creativity and determination often outweigh resources.
5. "I have to do it alone."
   - Success is rarely a solo journey. Seeking mentorship, collaboration, and support can accelerate progress. Surrounding yourself with the right people can make a huge difference.
6. "I'm too old/too young."
   - Age is not a barrier to success. Many people start new careers, businesses, or passions later in life, while others achieve great things at a young age. The key is taking action, regardless of age.
7. "I need to be perfect."

- Perfectionism can lead to paralysis. Success is about progress, not perfection. Taking imperfect action is better than waiting indefinitely for everything to be flawless.
8. "Success is only for lucky people."
    - Luck can play a role, but success is primarily built on effort, strategy, and persistence. Those who work hard and stay committed create their own opportunities. Luck is an excuse; faith is a doorway to impossibilities.

Breaking free from these limiting beliefs can open the door to new possibilities. Which of these resonates with you the most?

The Power of Renewing Your Mind:

Romans 12:2 teaches:

"Do not conform to the pattern of this world, but be transformed by the renewing of your mind."

Breaking free from limiting beliefs begins with renewing your mind—changing how you think and what you believe about yourself.

Ten power points on correct thinking:

1. God sees potential in you that you may not see yet.
    - Jeremiah 1:5 – Before I formed you in the womb I knew you...
    - Your identity is rooted in God's view, not your limitations.

2. Your past does not define your future.
   - 2 Corinthians 5:17 – If anyone is in Christ, he is a new creation...
   - A renewed mind accepts that grace rewrites your story.
3. You can't live a new life with an old mindset.
   - Romans 12:2 – Be transformed by the renewing of your mind...
   - Success starts with how you think – Transformation is internal before it is external.
4. The battlefield of success and faith is not in the wallet, but in the mind and heart.
   - 2 Corinthians 10:5 – Take every thought captive...
   - Winning in life requires mastering your thought life.
5. Fear is a liar; faith renews your perspective and core beliefs.
   - 2 Timothy 1:7 – God has not given us a spirit of fear...
   - A renewed mind chooses faith over fear, every time.
6. What you feed your mind determines your future.
   - Philippians 4:8 – Think on these things...
   - Fill your mind with truth, and your life will follow.
   - "What you eat, you become."
7. Your mindset sets the ceiling for your growth.
   - Success principle: Growth requires belief + strategy + consistency.
   - If you change your thinking, you change your results.
   - It was wisdom that brought the blessings of Israel through Solomon.
8. Agreement with God's Word is the starting point for breakthrough.
   - Amos 3:3 – "Can two walk together unless they agree..."

- A renewed mind agrees with heaven, not with past pain or doubt.
9. Identity precedes destiny.
    - Ephesians 2:10 – "Created in Christ Jesus for good works…"
    - A renewed mind accepts who you are in Christ before striving for what you do.
10. You don't have to be perfect to be powerful.
    - 2 Corinthians 12:9 – "My grace is sufficient for you, for my power is made perfect in weakness."
    - A renewed mind embraces progress over perfection – and relies on God's strength.

Taking Action: Breaking Free for Good

Once you recognize the limiting beliefs holding you back, you have to take action to break free:

1. Identify the Limiting Beliefs.
    - What thoughts have kept you small?
    - Write them down, and compare them to what God says about you in His Word.
    - The Holy Spirit can help us. Pray this simple prayer. "Lord, show me my limiting beliefs, or lies that are holding me back.
    - Now pray this, "Lord, where did this lie come from?"
    - Next, when He shows you, you may have to forgive yourself, or someone else. This brings freedom from the grip of the lie.
    - Ask God to set you free from the bondage of that lie. Then thank Him for revealing it and setting you free.

2. Speak Truth Over Your Life.
   - Proverbs 18:21 says, *"The tongue has the power of life and death."*
   - Stop agreeing with defeat. Start declaring God's promises over yourself.
   - Create a habit of healthy, productive thinking and speaking. Studies reflect that it takes one to two months to create a healthy habit. The words we speak shape the way we think. Neuroscience shows that positive affirmations and intentional language can create new neural pathways, rewiring our brains to foster confidence, resilience, and motivation. Over time, repeated positive speaking shifts behavior, helping us break free from self-doubt and step boldly into new possibilities.
3. Step Forward, Even if it's Scary.
   - Fear often looms larger in our minds than in reality. Some fears—like paper dragons—appear fierce but crumble the moment we confront them. When we step toward what scares us, we discover strength we didn't know we had. Facing fear reshapes our mindset, proving that courage isn't about being fearless—it's about acting despite the fear.
   - Action disrupts doubt. Start moving toward your dreams, even if the next step feels small.
   - Success is built on one choice at a time.

Your Future is Bigger Than Your Fear:

The only thing more dangerous than failure is never trying at all. You were not created for an average life—you were made for a purpose that impacts the world.

Your breakthrough begins when you refuse to believe the lie that you are stuck. The future is waiting. The question is—will you step into it?

Small Group Discussion – Chapter 10: *Freedom from Limiting Beliefs*

Key Verse:

"Do not conform to the pattern of this world, but be transformed by the renewing of your mind."
— Romans 12:2 (NIV)

Icebreaker Question:

What's one belief you had about yourself growing up that you've since realized wasn't true?

Discussion Questions:

1. Which limiting belief from the chapter do you personally relate to the most—and why?
   (Examples: "I'm not good enough," "I don't have the right resources," "I'm too old/too young")
2. What lie have you struggled to let go of that has held you back from stepping into God's purpose?
   How has it affected your decisions, confidence, or direction?
3. What stood out to you from the stories of Walt Disney, Joyce Meyer, or others?
   How did their mindset impact their journey?
4. How do you renew your mind with God's truth practically in daily life?

5. What scriptures, habits, or tools help you fight lies and speak truth?
6. Have you ever faced fear and acted anyway?
   What happened, and what did you learn about God—and yourself?

Action Step

Write one limiting belief you want to break free from this week. Then write a scripture-based truth to replace it.
Example:
Limiting Belief: *"I'm not qualified."*
Truth: *"God qualifies those He calls – Ephesians 2:10."*

Prayer Focus

Pray together for:

- Freedom from past lies and labels
- Courage to step into God's truth
- Renewed minds and confident hearts
- Boldness to pursue the dream He placed in each person

Next Step Challenge:

Speak life over yourself this week.
   Choose one truth statement (based on Scripture) and declare it out loud every morning. Watch how it shifts your mindset.

"Your mind is the steering wheel of your destiny—where it turns, your life will follow."

CHAPTER 11

PLAN AND CONQUER

"Give me six hours to chop down a tree and I will spend the first four sharpening the axe."

—Abraham Lincoln

Dreams don't build themselves. A business won't develop on its own, and a ministry doesn't just happen—they require intentional planning, strategy, and execution. Many people have great ideas, but never see them come to life because they fail to organize their vision into a clear, actionable plan.

Failing to plan is planning to fail.

Success isn't just about passion—it's about structure, discipline, and strategic thinking. Whether in business, ministry, or personal growth, those who master the art of planning are the ones who conquer their dreams.

> *Ecclesiastes 10:10 states: "If the axe is dull and one does not sharpen the edge, then he must use more strength; but wisdom brings success." (A good plan brings success.)*

Joseph's Strategic Planning in Egypt (Genesis 41)

One of the most powerful examples of planning and conquering in the Bible is Joseph's leadership in Egypt. In Genesis 41, Pharaoh had a troubling dream about seven years of abundance followed by seven years of famine. Joseph, through divine wisdom, interpreted the dream and immediately developed a strategic plan to prepare Egypt for the coming crisis.

Joseph didn't just hope for the best—he organized a nationwide food storage system, ensuring that grain was collected during the years of plenty and stored for the years of famine. His foresight and planning not only saved Egypt but also the surrounding nations, including his own family.

This story teaches us that our dreams will require preparation. Joseph's success wasn't just about his ability to interpret dreams—it was about his ability to plan, execute, and lead with wisdom.

The Power of Planning:

Planning is the bridge between vision and reality. Without a plan, dreams remain ideas—but with a plan, they become achievable goals. Proverbs 16:3 says: *"Commit to the Lord whatever you do, and He will establish your plans."* God blesses intentional effort. He gives vision, but He also expects us to steward that vision wisely through planning and execution.

Key Components of a Successful Plan

Every great plan includes five essential components:

1. Clear Vision – Define exactly what you want to achieve.

2. Strategic Goals – Break the vision into specific, measurable steps.
3. Resources & Team – Identify what you need and who can help.
4. Execution Strategy – Develop a timeline and action plan.
5. Accountability & Adaptation – Track progress and adjust as needed.

Biblical Examples of Strategic Planning

The Bible is filled with leaders who conquered their dreams through planning:

1. Nehemiah Rebuilding Jerusalem (Nehemiah 2:5-8). Nehemiah didn't just pray—he developed a plan, secured resources, and executed the rebuilding of Jerusalem.
2. Joseph Managing Egypt's Economy (Genesis 41:33-36). Joseph created a seven-year strategy to store grain and prevent famine, saving nations from disaster.
3. Jesus Training His Disciples (Luke 10:1-3). Jesus didn't randomly send His disciples—He strategically trained them, sent them in pairs, and gave them clear instructions.

CEOs Who Mastered Planning:

Successful business leaders don't rely on luck—they rely on strategy.

1. Steve Jobs (Apple). Jobs had a clear vision for Apple and meticulously planned product development, leading to revolutionary technology.

2. Jeff Bezos (Amazon). Bezos built Amazon through long-term strategic planning, focusing on customer experience and innovation.
3. Howard Schultz (Starbucks). Schultz developed a business plan that transformed Starbucks from a small coffee shop into a global brand.

Christian Leaders Who Built Ministries Through Planning:

Faith-based leaders also mastered the art of planning to fulfill their calling:

1. Billy Graham: Graham's evangelistic crusades weren't random—they were strategically planned, with teams organizing venues, outreach, and follow-up discipleship.
2. Rick Warren (Saddleback Church). Warren developed a structured church growth plan, leading Saddleback to become one of the most influential churches in the world.
3. Heidi Baker (Iris Global). Heidi Baker's ministry in Mozambique was built on strategic planning, including orphan care, church planting, and leadership training.

How to Develop Your Own Plan:

If you want to conquer your dream, follow these steps:

1. Dedicate the Dream to God. – Bathe your plan in prayer and fasting.
2. Write Down Your Vision (Habakkuk 2:2) – Define your dream clearly.

3. Set Specific Goals – Break it into achievable steps.
4. Identify Resources – What do you need? Who can help?
5. Create a Timeline – Set deadlines for each phase.
6. Stay Accountable – Track progress and adjust as needed.

If your dream is to build a business:

One of the most crucial steps you can take is creating a solid business plan. Many well-meaning entrepreneurs dive into startups with passion and ambition but fail to fully grasp the key factors that determine success—sales, overhead, payroll, competitor analysis, and financial forecasting. Without a clear roadmap, even the best ideas can struggle to gain traction.

A well-structured business plan is more than just a document—it's a strategic blueprint that guides decision-making, attracts investors, and ensures long-term sustainability.

Studies show that businesses with formal plans grow an estimated 30% faster than those without. Companies with well-defined plans are 2.5 times more likely to obtain funding, proving that structured planning is essential for financial stability. Additionally, 71% of successful small businesses have a documented business plan, proving that planning is a key ingredient in achieving stability and growth.

Research indicates that startups with business plans are 152% more likely to launch successfully. Additionally, 65% of businesses that stick to their plans achieve their strategic objectives, demonstrating the power of structured planning.

Consider the story of a young entrepreneur who dreamed of opening a coffee shop. Without a business plan, he struggled with budgeting, marketing, and inventory management. However, after stepping back and implementing a structured plan—including financial projections, competitor analysis, and a clear growth strategy—his business flourished, attracting investors and expanding to multiple locations.

Another example is a tech startup that nearly failed due to poor financial planning. Once the founders developed a detailed business plan, outlining revenue streams, cost structures, and market positioning, they secured funding and scaled their company successfully.

Key Elements of a Business Plan

A strong business plan includes several essential components:

- Executive Summary: A concise overview of your business, mission, and goals.
- Market Analysis: Research on industry trends, competitors, and target customers.
- Financial Projections: Revenue forecasts, budgeting, and funding strategies.
- Sales & Marketing Strategy: How you plan to attract and retain customers.
- Operational Plan: Logistics, staffing, and day-to-day business operations.
- Risk Assessment: Identifying potential challenges and strategies to overcome them.

Taking Action: Build Your Business Plan Today

If you're serious about launching a successful business, don't leave your future to chance. Download a business plan template and fill it out with intention. This single step can make the difference between struggling to survive and thriving in your industry.

If your dream is to build a ministry:

Churches and ministries that implement strategic planning experience higher engagement, financial stability, and long-term growth compared to those that operate without a clear direction.

Key Factors in Ministry Planning:

A successful ministry plan should address several critical areas:

1. Defining Your Mission & Vision. Every ministry must start with a clear mission statement—a concise declaration of its purpose.
    - What is the core mission of this ministry?
    - Who are we called to serve?
    - What impact do we want to make?
2. Growth Strategy: How Will You Expand? Growth doesn't happen by chance—it requires intentional outreach and engagement. Consider:
    - Community Engagement: Hosting events, outreach programs, and service initiatives.
    - Digital Presence: Leveraging social media, websites, and online sermons.
    - Discipleship Programs: Small groups, Bible studies, and mentorship opportunities.
3. Attracting & Retaining People: Getting people into your church is one thing—keeping them engaged is another. Strategies include:
    - Welcoming Culture: First impressions matter. Train greeters and create a warm environment.

- Follow-Up System: Connect with visitors through calls, emails, or personal invitations.
- Meaningful Worship & Teaching: Ensure sermons are relevant, engaging, and biblically sound.
- Opportunities for Involvement: Encourage participation in ministries, volunteer roles, and leadership development.

4. Leadership & Roles: Who Does What? A ministry thrives when responsibilities are clearly defined. Key roles include:
   - Lead Pastor/Minister: Oversees vision, teaching, and spiritual direction.
   - Small Group or Cell Leadership Team: Leads and plants new small groups.
   - Administrative Team: Manages finances, scheduling, and logistics.
   - Outreach & Evangelism Team: Focuses on community engagement and growth.
   - Worship & Media Team: Leads music, production, and digital outreach.
   - Discipleship & Care Team: Supports spiritual growth and pastoral care.

4. Financial Planning: Counting the Cost. Ministry requires financial stewardship.
   Consider:
   - Budgeting: Salaries, building costs, outreach expenses, and operational needs.
   - Fundraising & Giving: Tithes, offerings, sponsorships, and grants.
   - Long-Term Sustainability: Planning for future expansion, staff growth, and unexpected expenses.

5. Long-Term Vision & Goals. A ministry should have short-term and long-term goals to measure progress. Examples:
   - Short-Term: Increase attendance, launch a new outreach program, improve online presence.
   - Long-Term: Build a new facility, expand to multiple locations, and develop leadership training programs.
6. What Keeps People in a Ministry? Retention is key to a thriving ministry.
   Factors include:
   - Authentic Relationships: People stay where they feel valued and connected.
   - Spiritual Growth Opportunities: Bible studies, mentorship, and discipleship programs.
   - Purpose & Involvement: Giving members meaningful roles and responsibilities.
   - Strong Leadership & Vision: A clear direction keeps people engaged and motivated.

A ministry without a plan is like a ship without a rudder—it may move, but it won't reach its destination. By defining your mission, creating a growth strategy, managing finances wisely, and fostering engagement, your ministry can flourish and make a lasting impact.

Your Dream Needs a Plan:

Remember, someday never comes—but with a well-crafted plan, your dream can become a reality. Take the reins, structure your plan, and set yourself up for success.

Are you ready to take the next step?

Small Group Lesson: Chapter 11: Plan and Conquer

Theme Scripture:

"Commit to the Lord whatever you do, and He will establish your plans."

—Proverbs 16:3 (NIV)

Icebreaker Question:

Have you ever had a great idea or dream that didn't happen? What stopped it from moving forward?

Main Point:

Big dreams require bold faith *and* intentional planning. God gives the vision, but we must develop the structure to see it come to life.

Key Insight:

"Give me six hours to chop down a tree and I will spend the first four sharpening the axe."

—Abraham Lincoln

Great success starts with great preparation.

Like Joseph in Egypt (Genesis 41), your ability to plan can protect your purpose, unlock opportunities, and serve others. Planning isn't just practical—it's biblical.

Discussion Questions:

1. What's a dream God has placed in your heart that you haven't fully planned for?
2. How do you currently approach planning—are you strategic or spontaneous?
3. In what areas of your life or calling do you need better structure?
4. How does involving God in your plans change your confidence and outcomes?

Action Steps:

- Dedicate the Dream: Start with prayer. Ask God to guide and bless your planning.
- Write the Vision: Identify your goal and write it down (Habakkuk 2:2).
- Break It Down: List three steps you can take this month toward your dream.
- Find Accountability: Share your plan with someone in the group who can help you stay on track.

Prayer:

Lord, thank You for the dreams You've placed in our hearts. Give us the wisdom to plan, the discipline to execute, and the faith to believe You'll guide every step. Teach us to be faithful stewards of the vision You've given us. In Jesus' name, amen.

CHAPTER 12

ONE SMALL STEP FOR MAN, ONE LARGE STEP TOWARD DREAM FULFILLMENT

"That's one small step for man, one giant leap for mankind."
—Neil Armstrong, July 20, 1969

On a quiet July night in 1969, millions watched as Neil Armstrong descended a ladder and placed his boot on the surface of the moon. It was a breathtaking moment—not just for space exploration, but for the power of bold beginnings. The moon landing didn't happen overnight. It was the result of years of planning, preparation, setbacks, and sacrifice. But none of it would have mattered without that first courageous step.

Just like the Apollo 11 mission, our dreams require us to launch—often without seeing the entire path. Whether you're building a business, stepping into ministry, or chasing a God-given goal, the greatest progress begins with the smallest movement forward. The unknown may feel intimidating, but every leap of faith starts with one step of obedience.

The journey of a thousand miles—and the fulfillment of your calling—starts not with certainty, but with courage.

Every great achievement begins with one small step. Whether it's launching a business, stepping into ministry, or pursuing a lifelong dream, the hardest part is often getting started. Fear, doubt, and hesitation can feel overwhelming, but taking the first step is the key to unlocking your destiny.

The Power of the First Step:

Lao Tzu famously said, *"The journey of a thousand miles begins with one step."*

This truth applies to every dream, every goal, and every breakthrough. The first step may feel small, but it carries immense power—it sets everything in motion.

Quotes to Inspire Your First Step:

- *"Faith is taking the first step even when you don't see the whole staircase."*—Martin Luther King Jr.
- *"The secret of getting ahead is getting started."*—Mark Twain
- *"You don't have to be great to start, but you have to start to be great."*—Zig Ziglar
- *"The most important step of all is the first step. Start something."*—Blake Mycoskie

Biblical Stories of Taking the First Step

The moon landing wasn't achieved in a single leap—it began with a risky, calculated, and courageous first step. The same is true in the Kingdom of God. Every act of destiny in Scripture began with someone who dared to step forward in the face of fear, uncertainty, and impossibility.

1. Peter Walking on Water (Matthew 14:29)

The storm was raging. The boat rocked violently. Most people would have clung tighter to safety—but Peter saw Jesus walking on the waves and said, "Lord, if it's You, tell me to come." Jesus simply replied, "Come."

Peter didn't wait for the sea to calm or for assurance he wouldn't sink—he stepped out in faith. That moment became the only recorded instance of a man walking on water. Though he faltered, he walked further than those who stayed behind.

- Key Insight: Miracles often lie on the other side of movement. The boat feels safer, but staying in it means missing what God is doing on the water. Peter teaches us that imperfect faith is better than perfect inaction.

2. Abraham Leaving His Homeland (Genesis 12:1)

Abraham was comfortable. He had family, land, and security. Then God disrupted his life with a calling: "Leave your country, your people, and your father's household . . . to a land I will show you."

No directions. No guarantee. Just a promise. Abraham had to let go of what he knew to receive what God had planned. His simple obedience birthed a lineage that would bless the world.

- Key Insight: Great destinies are unlocked by people willing to leave the familiar. Abraham shows us that God doesn't show the whole map—He shows the next step. Faith isn't knowing the destination—it's trusting the One who guides the journey.

3. David Facing Goliath (1 Samuel 17:45–47)

David wasn't a soldier—he was a shepherd boy. Goliath was a seasoned warrior. The entire army of Israel stood frozen in fear, yet David stepped forward with nothing but a sling and five smooth stones.

His courage wasn't in his weapon—it was in his belief that God was bigger than the giant. David's decision to step onto that battlefield didn't just change his life; it set the course for Israel's victory and his future kingship.

- Key Insight: The first step toward your destiny may be the scariest, but it can change the outcome for everyone around you. David didn't wait for someone stronger to rise up—he moved forward and showed that faith can defeat what fear cannot face.

These stories show us that the first step is often the hardest—but it's also the most transformational. Like Neil Armstrong stepping off the lunar module onto uncharted ground, Peter, Abraham, and David each had a "moon landing" moment where they had to silence fear and step into purpose.

God doesn't call the fearless—He calls the faithful. And He's waiting for you to take that first step.

How to Take Your First Step:

If you're struggling to start, here's how to break through hesitation:

1. Decide Today – Stop waiting for the perfect moment. Start now.
2. Break It Down – Focus on one small action instead of the entire journey.
3. Create a schedule with deadlines – A schedule will help you make progress.
4. Silence Fear – Fear will always try to stop you. Move forward anyway.
5. Start where you're at – Make it good, then make it great!
6. Find Support – Surround yourself with people who encourage your dream.
7. Trust God – Step out in faith, knowing that God will guide you.

Your Future Begins with One Step:

No matter how big your dream is, it starts with one decision, one action, one step. The difference between those who succeed and those who stay stuck is simple—the ones who succeed take the first step.

Are you ready to step into your destiny?

Small Group Lesson: Chapter 12: One Small Step for Man, One Giant Leap Toward Dream Fulfillment

"That's one small step for man, one giant leap for mankind."

—NEIL ARMSTRONG, JULY 20, 1969

Big Idea:

Just like the moon landing required years of planning followed by one bold step into the unknown, your God-given dream will never lift off until you take action. Fear will always whisper, "Not yet," but progress begins with obedience. One step forward can change everything.

Key Scripture:

Matthew 14:29 — *"Then Peter got down out of the boat, walked on the water and came toward Jesus."*

Genesis 12:1 — *"Go from your country, your people and your father's household to the land I will show you."*

1 Samuel 17:45 — *"You come against me with sword and spear ... but I come against you in the name of the Lord Almighty."*

Bible Snapshots of Bold First Steps:

1. Peter Walked on Water (Matt. 14:29)
   In the middle of a storm, Peter stepped out while others stayed safe.
   - *Faith moves before clarity arrives. You won't walk on water if you never leave the boat.*
2. Abraham Left Everything (Gen. 12:1)
   Abraham obeyed God without a map, stepping into the unknown.
   - *The journey to promise begins with trust, not directions.*
3. David Faced Goliath (1 Sam. 17:45–47)
   David ran toward the giant while trained warriors stood frozen.
   - *Your first step may feel small, but it can shake nations.*

Group Discussion:

1. What "first step" is God prompting you to take right now?
2. What's keeping you in the "boat" of comfort or fear?
3. Which of the three biblical figures inspires you most—and why?
4. Think of a past moment when taking a first step led to breakthrough. What did you learn?

Launch Checklist: How to Take Your First Step

- Decide Today – Don't wait for perfect conditions.
- Take a Micro-Step – Start with something simple and actionable.

- Silence Fear – Trust God more than your feelings.
- Share It – Tell someone what you're stepping into.
- Pray Boldly – Invite God to lead every step.

Closing Prayer:

"Father, thank You for calling us to greater things. Give us the courage to step forward, even when the path isn't fully clear. Like Peter, Abraham, and David, may we trust You enough to move. We don't need to see the whole staircase—just the next step. In Jesus' name, Amen."

CHAPTER 13

TIME MANAGEMENT, TAMING THE WILD STALLION

"Lost time is never found again."
—*Benjamin Franklin*

Taming Time: The Wild Stallion of Productivity

Growing up, I was captivated by horses. My aunt's home in Reeve, Wisconsin, was a haven where the rhythmic beat of hooves and the scent of fresh hay filled the air. She had several horses—some gentle and steady, others untamed and unpredictable. We would ride for hours through the rolling countryside, feeling the strength of the animals beneath us. It was a kind of heaven.

Among the most exhilarating moments of my childhood were those spent watching classic John Wayne movies. There was always a young ranch hand tasked with breaking a wild stallion. The first ride was always chaotic—the horse bucking, kicking, and doing everything in its power to throw off the rider. But the ranch hand didn't give up. With grit, patience, and unshakable resolve, he held on. Eventually, the stallion tired, realizing its days of wild freedom were over. Instead of being conquered, it was transformed—no longer a force of chaos, but a disciplined, powerful, and productive creature.

Time is much the same. It is wild and unpredictable. If left untamed, it slips through our fingers, galloping into the distance, leaving us staring in its wake, wondering where the days, weeks, and years have gone. But just as a skilled horse trainer can break a mustang, we, too, can harness time—guiding it with discipline, purpose, and intentionality.

Breaking the Wild Stallion Called Time:

So, what's the secret to taming time? It starts with control. A horse isn't broken in a day, and neither is a chaotic schedule. The process requires patience, consistency, and a firm but steady grip.

The ranch hand knows the key isn't simply holding on—it's strategic guidance, clear boundaries, and unwavering discipline. Time, too, must be handled with intention. Without structure, our days blur into weeks, our weeks into months. The hours slip away, wasted on distractions, until suddenly, entire seasons of life have vanished.

A schedule is the reins that guide time, helping us shape our days with purpose.

Some claim that individuals who structure their time effectively are 42% more productive than those who don't. The most successful people don't leave their time to chance; they train it, just as the ranch hand trains the horse. They wake up early, prioritize important tasks, and remain committed to their goals.

- "Time is what we want most, but what we use worst."—*William Penn*
- "The key is in not spending time, but in investing it."—*Stephen R. Covey*
- "You may delay, but time will not."—*Benjamin Franklin*
- "The bad news is time flies. The good news is you're the pilot."—*Michael Altshuler*

The Power of Scheduling and Routine

Just as breaking a horse requires patience and consistency, mastering time demands discipline. Today, we have an incredible tool at our fingertips—our cell phone calendars. These aren't just for scheduling meetings; they have the potential to transform our lives, helping us stay on track and bring our dreams to life.

When I was a young executive, the company I worked for wanted to improve office productivity. To achieve this, they hired a team of consultants to evaluate our workflows and help us reach our goals. After several weeks of observation, the consultants presented a strategy that was surprisingly simple but profoundly effective.

They trained every office worker in a new system built around a daily structure and consistent habits. Once we implemented the changes, the results were immediate and impressive. Customer issues stopped slipping through the cracks, meetings started on time, notes were organized and easy to access, and daily tasks were clearly prioritized. As a result, customer complaints dropped—and sales went up.

We implemented a few simple yet highly effective strategies that had a remarkable impact. If you apply these principles to your personal and professional life, they can significantly increase your chances of success.

1. Use a Daily Planner (Paper or Digital). Each employee was issued a planner that included:
   - A dated page for every workday
   - A to-do list with prioritized tasks
   - Notes section for projects and customer issues
   - A monthly overview for long-term scheduling
   - Every morning, the first ten minutes were dedicated to updating the planner:
     A. Review and Transfer Notes: Go through the previous day's notes and identify any unresolved issues. Transfer those to the current day's to-do list and make sure nothing slips through the cracks.
     B. Prioritize the To-Do List: Add, remove, or adjust items based on current needs. Assign each task a priority number (1–4), with 1 being the highest. Level 1 tasks—urgent client issues, time-sensitive projects—had to be addressed first.
     C. Update the Daily Schedule: Include meetings, appointments, blocks of time for deep work, and client follow-ups. Treat time slots like immovable commitments.
     D. Manage the Monthly Calendar: Track business travel, upcoming deadlines, vacation days, and long-term goals. Planning ahead helped reduce last-minute stress.

2. Review and Organize All Digital Communication: Before diving into tasks, employees were trained to scan through emails and messages:
   - Flag anything requiring action or follow-up
   - Archive or delete clutter
   - Respond to anything quickly, and schedule time for lengthier responses
   - This helped everyone start their day with a clear inbox and focused mind.
3. Eliminate Distractions:
   Small interruptions cause major inefficiencies. Employees learned to:
   - Silence unnecessary notifications
   - Use headphones or closed doors to signal "do not disturb" during deep work
   - Limit social media and personal browsing to scheduled breaks
4. Schedule Breaks Intentionally:
   Rather than working through fatigue, short breaks were built into the schedule to reset and recharge—improving focus over the long run.
5. End-of-Day Review:
   At the end of each day, team members would spend five minutes:
   - Reviewing what was accomplished
   - Marking incomplete items for follow-up
   - Preparing their planner for the next morning

When employees consistently followed these time management practices, productivity soared. Customer issues were addressed quickly, tasks were completed on time, and employees felt more in control of their workload. The key wasn't just working harder—it was working smarter through structure and discipline.

Studies have shown that college students and young professionals who implement structured planning, goal-setting, and prioritization techniques significantly outperform their peers. Time is unforgiving to those who let it run wild—but it becomes a powerful ally when properly harnessed.

The choice is ours: Will we let time slip away, or will we take the reins?

Late Nights vs. Early Mornings

One of the key debates in time management is whether staying up late or waking up early yields more productivity. Research suggests that early risers tend to be more proactive and successful. The Bible reflects this wisdom: *"She rises while it is yet night and provides food for her household"* (Proverbs 31:15).

Waking up early provides a sense of control—quiet moments to plan, reflect, and focus before the world demands our attention. Many of the most productive individuals tackle their most important work before 8:00 AM, proving that time favors the disciplined.

Work Hard and Manage Your Time: The Foundation of Progress

Discipline and planning mean nothing without effort. Throughout history, people have built extraordinary lives through focused, hard work.

- "There is no substitute for hard work."—Thomas Edison

- "Hard work beats talent when talent doesn't work hard."—Tim Notke

Sylvester Stallone's story is a perfect example. Homeless and broke, he refused to give up. He sold his dog to survive. He decided to dedicate his time to writing. With great focused effort, he wrote *Rocky* in three days and insisted on playing the lead. Despite rejection, he persevered. The result? One of the greatest underdog stories in cinematic history.

Balancing Work and Family

Hard work is noble, but not if it comes at the expense of your health or relationships.

> "In vain you rise early and stay up late . . . for He grants sleep to those He loves."
> —Psalm 127:2

Make time for rest. Honor the Sabbath. Cherish your family. The most productive life is also the most balanced.

Biblical Wisdom on Time Management

Time is one of the most valuable resources we have—it's finite, fleeting, and once lost, it can never be regained. The Bible offers profound guidance on how we should steward this gift with wisdom, diligence, and purpose.

> "Teach us to number our days, that we may gain a heart of wisdom."
> —Psalm 90:12

This verse reminds us that our time on earth is limited, and because of that, we must live with a sense of urgency and purpose. When we understand that our days are numbered, we begin to prioritize what truly matters—relationships, calling, service, and obedience to God. Numbering our days isn't about counting them—it's about making them count.

"Whatever you do, work at it with all your heart, as working for the Lord, not for human masters."—Colossians 3:23

This passage elevates everyday tasks to acts of worship. Whether you're working in an office, leading a ministry, raising a family, or studying for exams—your work matters to God. Time management isn't just a productivity tool; it's a way to honor God through our effort and commitment. Doing your best is a form of worship when it's done for the Lord.

Why God Cares About Our Time:

- Time reveals our priorities. How we spend our time shows what we truly value. God desires to be first in our lives, and that includes how we allocate our schedule.
- Time reflects our obedience. Ephesians 5:15-16 says, *"Be very careful, then, how you live—not as unwise but as wise, making the most of every opportunity, because the days are evil."* We are called to redeem the time, to use it wisely in a world that constantly pulls us toward distraction and waste.
- Time is part of our witness. The world watches how believers live. A disciplined, focused, and purpose-driven life speaks volumes about our faith and our God.

Stewardship of Time: Practical Application

- Start the day with God. Spend time in prayer, Scripture, or reflection to align your priorities before the busyness begins.
- Set boundaries. Learn to say no to things that waste time or pull you away from your calling.
- Rest intentionally. God created the Sabbath as a rhythm of renewal. Taking time to rest isn't laziness—it's obedience.
- Be present. Time management isn't just about doing more—it's about being fully engaged in what matters most.

In the end, time isn't just a resource to manage—it's a sacred trust to steward. And the way we manage our time says more about our faith than we may realize. When we submit our schedules to God, He multiplies our impact, strengthens our purpose, and ensures that none of our days are wasted.

Conclusion: Take the Reins

Time may never be perfectly tamed, but it can be mastered. Like the wild stallion, it must be trained with consistency, clarity, and conviction.

Your life is too valuable to leave to chance. Will you let time run wild—or will you take the reins?

Small Group Lesson: Chapter 13: Taming Time – Taking the Reins

Theme Scripture:

"Teach us to number our days, that we may gain a heart of wisdom."

—Psalm 90:12 (NIV)

Big Idea:

Time, like a wild stallion, must be tamed—not controlled with brute force, but trained with discipline, structure, and purpose. When we master time, we multiply our impact in business, ministry, and life.

Opening Discussion:

- On a scale of 1 to 10, how well would you say you manage your time?
- What is one area of your life where time feels out of control?

Key Bible Insight:

"A little sleep, a little slumber . . . and poverty will come on you like a thief."

—Proverbs 6:10-11

God calls us to steward time wisely. Like the ranch hand breaking a wild stallion, we must take hold of our schedules and guide our days intentionally—before life runs away from us.

Three Principles to Tame the Stallion of Time:

1. Structure Wins the Day
   Time-block your calendar. Use your phone or planner to schedule what matters most—prayer, work, family, rest.
2. Prioritize What Matters
   Apply the *Eisenhower Matrix*: Urgent vs. Important. Focus on tasks that move your dream forward—not just the loudest distractions.
3. Start Your Day Early
   Proverbs 31:15 reminds us that wisdom wakes early. Mornings offer focus and clarity. Use them to dream, plan, pray, and act.

Activity: Time Audit Exercise

Take five minutes to write down how you spent your last 24 hours.

- Where did time get wasted?
- What could be restructured or delegated?
- What time block will you commit to your dream this week?

Quotes for Motivation:

- "Don't wait. The time will never be just right."—*Napoleon Hill*
- "Hard work beats talent when talent doesn't work hard." —*Tim Notke*

- *"I'm a great believer in luck, and I find the harder I work, the more I have of it."—Thomas Jefferson*

Challenge This Week:

Pick one time management habit to practice daily—whether it's waking up earlier, using your calendar, or prioritizing your top three tasks. Take the reins before time runs away.

Prayer: Have the group pray and ask God to help each person manage their time so that they can achieve all that God has for them.

CHAPTER 14

TAKING RISKS – WALKING ON WATER

"Only those who will risk going too far can possibly find out how far one can go."

—T.S. Eliot

Every breakthrough begins at the edge of your comfort zone. Risk isn't a reckless leap—it's a step of courage into the unknown. It's where faith becomes action and vision becomes reality.

Taking a risk is often the difference between a dream that stays dormant and one that comes to life. Whether in faith, business, or personal growth, risk is the currency of forward motion.

Peter Walks on Water: A Biblical Blueprint

In Matthew 14, the disciples are caught in a storm when they see Jesus walking on the water. Peter calls out, "Lord, if it's you, tell me to come to you on the water." Jesus replies with one word: "Come." Peter steps out. He walks on water—not because he had a plan, but because he had faith. Yes, he began to sink when he saw the wind—but Jesus reached out and caught him.

Peter didn't fail—he walked further than anyone else because he was willing to risk the boat. The rest of the disciples stayed safe—and missed the miracle.

Faith always requires a step. Risk is the evidence that you're walking in it.

Business Risk: Jan Koum – From Food Stamps to WhatsApp

Jan Koum, co-founder of WhatsApp, grew up in Ukraine and later lived on food stamps after immigrating to the U.S. He taught himself programming and landed a job at Yahoo. But in 2009, he quit that stable job to pursue a dream—building a simple, private messaging app.

For years, Koum and his co-founder faced failure, funding the project themselves. He was even rejected for a job at Facebook. Ironically, Facebook would later buy WhatsApp for $19 billion.

Koum's willingness to risk stability for innovation turned him from a struggling immigrant into a global tech leader. His story proves: The right risk can rewrite your future.

Sports Risk: Giannis Antetokounmpo – Betting on Potential

Giannis Antetokounmpo grew up in extreme poverty in Greece, helping his parents by selling goods on the street. With no connections and barely speaking English, he entered the NBA draft—risking everything on a dream.

The risk paid off. Today, he's a two-time MVP and NBA Champion known as "The Greek Freak." Giannis didn't wait for certainty—he believed in his potential when no one else fully saw it. That kind of boldness transforms lives.

Ministry Risk: Abraham's Journey

In Genesis 12, God tells Abraham to leave his home and go "to the land I will show you." No map. No details. Just a call.

Abraham obeyed—and from that obedience came the birth of a nation. The promise was fulfilled because he said yes without knowing how. He risked familiarity for faith—and God honored it.

When God calls, He rarely gives all the details. Faith means moving before you see the finish line.

Why Most People Avoid Risk—And Why You Can't:

People don't avoid risk because they're incapable. They avoid it because of fear—fear of failure, fear of embarrassment, fear of loss. But staying safe is its own kind of risk: the risk of never growing, never changing, never living fully.

Here's what we know:

- Over 50% of startups fail within five years.
- Most high achievers have failed multiple times before succeeding.

Key Truths About Taking Risks

- Faith isn't the absence of fear—it's action in spite of it.

- Failure isn't final—it's a lesson on the way to success.
- You don't need full clarity to start—you need obedience.
- God meets you in motion, not in hesitation.

Reflection Questions:

- Where is God calling you to step out in faith?
- What fear is holding you back?
- What plan must you create to alleviate your fear?
- What would one bold step look like this week?

Risk the Water:

Every great entrepreneur, leader, athlete, or minister you admire all have one thing in common: they were willing to take a risk. They didn't wait for guarantees. They moved when the moment came.

Risk isn't the enemy—fear is. Playing it safe may feel comfortable, but it never leads to transformation.

Practical Takeaway: What's Your Boat?

Just like Peter, there's a boat you're sitting in. It might be comfort, security, routine, or even fear. What would happen if you stepped out? What dream is waiting on the other side of your risk?

- "If you want something you've never had, you have to do something you've never done."

Reflection Questions:

- What's one area where you feel God calling you to take a risk?

- What fear is holding you back—and what would courage look like this week?
- Are you willing to fail forward, trusting that God uses every step?

Take the Risk:

Every giant of faith, every successful entrepreneur, every record-breaking athlete—they all took a chance. They didn't wait for perfect conditions. They moved when they felt the call, and they figured out the rest along the way.

- Your dream won't happen by accident.
- Your future is on the other side of fear.
- You have to choose the risk, take the step, and trust that God meets you in motion.

Every great achievement requires risk. Whether in business, sports, or ministry, those who succeed are often the ones who step out in faith, take calculated risks, and refuse to let fear hold them back. Risk is not recklessness—it is strategic courage, the willingness to move forward despite uncertainty.

The Power of Risk in Business

Many of the world's most successful entrepreneurs risked everything to build their empires.

Donald Trump – Risking It All in Real Estate

Before becoming a household name, Donald Trump took massive risks in real estate. He leveraged loans, made bold investments, and built skyscrapers when others doubted his vision. His willingness to take financial risks led to the creation of Trump Tower, casinos, and luxury properties that shaped his empire.

Elon Musk – Betting His Fortune on Tesla and SpaceX

Elon Musk invested nearly all his money into Tesla and SpaceX, risking bankruptcy. At one point, both companies were on the verge of collapse, but Musk refused to quit. His bold risk-taking led to Tesla revolutionizing the auto industry and SpaceX pioneering private space travel.

Sara Blakely – Risking Her Savings to Create Spanx

Sara Blakely, the founder of Spanx, invested her entire life savings into developing her product. She faced rejection from manufacturers and retailers, but her persistence paid off—Spanx became a billion-dollar brand.

Risk in Sports: Athletes Who Took Bold Steps

Athletes must take risks to push their limits, break records, and achieve greatness.

Michael Jordan – Leaving Basketball for Baseball

At the peak of his career, Michael Jordan took a huge risk—leaving basketball to pursue baseball. Though his baseball career was short-lived, his willingness to step into the unknown proved his fearless mindset.

Tom Brady – Betting on Himself

Tom Brady was drafted as the 199th pick, overlooked by nearly every team. Instead of accepting mediocrity, he took risks in training, leadership, and performance, becoming one of the greatest quarterbacks in history.

Risk in Ministry: Leaders Who Stepped Out in Faith

Ministry requires boldness and trust in God. Many pastors and missionaries risked everything to follow their calling.

Billy Graham – Preaching to Empty Stadiums

Before becoming a world-renowned evangelist, Billy Graham preached to small crowds. He took the risk of organizing massive crusades, trusting that God would bring the people. His faith led to millions hearing the Gospel.

Heidi Baker – Risking Everything for Missions

Heidi Baker moved to Mozambique with no financial security, trusting God to provide. She faced poverty, opposition, and danger, but her risk led to thousands of churches planted and countless lives transformed.

Statistics on Business Ventures and Financial Risks: Risk is Real.

Starting a business is one of the biggest financial risks a person can take. However, if you have an excellent business plan, goals, and discipline, you can grow a thriving business. Planning matters. Here are some key statistics I've gleaned and produced estimates on business failures:

- Exploding Topics (2025) states that 10% of startups fail in the first year, but failure rates increase significantly over time, with 70% failing within five years.
- Forbes Advisor (2024) reports that 20% of startups fail within the first year, and 50% fail within five years.
- Failory (2024) notes that 9 out of 10 startups fail overall, with tech startups having one of the highest failure rates.
- Bureau of Labor Statistics data suggests that 65% of startups fail within ten years.

The Benefits of Taking Risks in Business

While risk can feel intimidating, strategic risk-taking is often the key to success. Many of the world's most successful entrepreneurs didn't play it safe—they stepped out, took calculated risks, and built businesses that transformed their lives and their families.

How Risk Leads to Growth:

Taking risks in business isn't about recklessness—it's about bold, informed decision-making. Studies show that:
- Entrepreneurs who take calculated risks are more likely to build sustainable businesses.
- Small business owners create financial stability for their families, often earning more than traditional employees over time.
- Businesses that innovate and take strategic risks tend to outperform competitors and adapt better to market changes.

Financial Benefits for Families:

A successful business doesn't just impact the owner—it creates opportunities for their family:

- Generational wealth – A thriving business can provide long-term financial security, allowing families to invest in homes, education, and future ventures.
- Flexibility and independence – Business owners often have more control over their schedules, creating a better work-life balance.
- Legacy building – Many entrepreneurs pass their businesses down to their children, ensuring financial stability for future generations.

Risk-Taking Fuels Innovation:

Every major breakthrough in business has come from someone willing to take a risk:

- Amazon disrupted retail by betting on e-commerce when others doubted it.
- Tesla revolutionized the auto industry by taking a chance on electric vehicles.
- Netflix transformed entertainment by shifting from DVDs to streaming.

Without risk, there is no innovation, no progress, and no breakthrough success.

The Key: Calculated Risk

The difference between failure and success isn't avoiding risk—it's taking the right risks. Smart entrepreneurs:

- Research before making big decisions.
- Surround themselves with mentors and advisors.
- Adapt quickly when challenges arise.
- Stay committed to their vision despite uncertainty.

Taking risks in business can be life-changing, not just financially but in purpose, freedom, and impact.

What's Your Boat?

Peter had to step out of the boat to experience the miraculous. What's your boat? What's keeping you from stepping out? Is it a stable job? A fear of rejection? The comfort of routine? Whatever it is, ask yourself: "What dream is waiting on the other side of my risk?" "If you want something you've never had, you must be willing to do something you've never done." - Attributed to Thomas Jefferson

Small Group Lesson — Chapter 14: Taking Risks – Walking on Water

Key Verse:

"Then Peter got down out of the boat, walked on the water and came toward Jesus."

—Matthew 14:29 (NIV)

Big Idea:

Taking risks in faith is how we step into our calling. Whether it's launching a business, pursuing a dream, or saying yes to God's leading—true growth happens when we leave the boat.

Opening Discussion

- What's the biggest risk you've ever taken?
- How did it shape who you are today?

Bible Focus: Matthew 14:22–33 (Peter Walks on Water)

Read together. Then discuss:

- What stands out to you in Peter's response to Jesus?
- Why do you think the other disciples stayed in the boat?
- How do you relate to Peter's courage—or his fear?

Key Point:

Peter didn't fail—he walked on water. He saw the impossible become possible *because* he took the step.

Real-Life Risk Stories (Brief Summaries):

- **Business:** *Jan Koum*, co-founder of WhatsApp, quit a stable job to build a risky startup. He ended up creating a $19 billion platform.
- **Sports:** *Giannis Antetokounmpo* left poverty and everything familiar to pursue the NBA. He's now an MVP.
- **Faith:** *Abraham* left his home on nothing but a promise from God—and became the father of a nation.

Question:
What do these stories have in common with Peter?

Group Reflection

Ask:
1. What "boat" are you currently sitting in? (Comfort zone, fear, stability?)
2. What risk is God prompting you to take?
3. What would one bold step of faith look like this week?

Key Takeaways:

- Faith isn't the absence of fear—it's obedience in the middle of it.
- God rarely gives full instructions—just an invitation: "Come."
- Failure isn't fatal. Playing it safe can be.

Scriptures to Reflect On:

- *Hebrews 11:6* — "Without faith it is impossible to please God..."
- *Romans 1:17* — "The righteous will live by faith."
- *Genesis 12:1–4* — God calls Abraham to go...with no details.

Challenge for the Week:

Identify one area where you need to take a faith-filled risk. Write it down. Take one action step toward it this week.

Closing Prayer:

Ask God for courage to leave the boat, faith to walk through fear, and boldness to pursue the call on your life—even when it means stepping into the unknown.

CHAPTER 15
TRUE SUCCESS

"But remember the LORD your God, for it is he who gives you the ability to produce wealth."
—*Deuteronomy 8:18*

My desire is to see you become successful—not just in the eyes of the world, but in the fullness of who God created you to be. You have greatness within you. With focus, faith, and intentional action, you can achieve more than you ever imagined. True success isn't just about money or status—it's about living a life of purpose, balance, and lasting impact. It's about using your gifts to make a difference, leaving a legacy that outlives you. My hope is that this chapter ignites something in you—a fresh vision, a deeper conviction, and the boldness to chase your dreams with everything you've got.

What is Success?

Success is one of the most misunderstood concepts in our world today. Society often equates success with wealth, status, and recognition, but true success goes far beyond material achievements.

Success is not about comparison, but about purpose. It's not about chasing riches, but about faithfulness. Success is found in following the path God has set before you, using your gifts to serve others, and walking in obedience to His calling.

Real success isn't measured by what you possess, but by what you give—your time, wisdom, encouragement, and service to others.

Ask Yourself:

- Am I living for purpose, or just chasing possessions?
- Am I measuring success by God's standards, or by the world's expectations?
- Am I focused on helping others grow, or just advancing myself?
- Am I using God's blessing to bless others?

Success is not a destination—it's a life lived with meaning. Pursue purpose, serve others, and trust God's plan, and you will walk in true success.

Success is Fulfilling Your Purpose:

Dr. Myles Munroe, a renowned leadership teacher, taught that success is not measured by money or fame, but by fulfilling your God-given purpose. He said:

"Success is not a comparison of what we have done with what others have done. Success is the fulfillment of purpose."

Success is Serving Others:

Similarly, Zig Ziglar, one of the greatest motivational speakers of all time, emphasized that success is not just about career accomplishments, but about living a life of integrity, faith, and service. His famous quote reflects this truth:

> *"You can have everything in life you want if you will just help enough other people get what they want."*

Zig understood that true success is found in helping others succeed. His philosophy was rooted in generosity, wisdom, and biblical principles.

A Personal Encounter With Zig Ziglar:

I had the privilege of meeting Zig Ziglar around 2005 after a conference. Despite his fame and influence, he was incredibly personable. He treated me like I was important, engaged in conversation, and never carried an air of superiority. What struck me most was his humility—despite his global recognition, he gave all the credit to Christ. He lived what he preached, embodying success through service and faith rather than status or riches.

Money is Not Evil:

Somewhere along the way—possibly during a long sermon in a hot church with no air conditioning—people began to equate wealth with wickedness. Perhaps it was a misquote of 1 Timothy 6:10, which says, *"The love of money is the root of all evil."* Notice—it doesn't say money itself is evil. It's the *love* of money, the obsession with it, that leads people down the wrong path.

Let's clear this up: Money is a tool, not a temptation. It's like a hammer—you can build a house with it, or you can break a window. It all depends on whose hand it's in and what their heart intends to do with it.

With the right motives, money is a powerful force for good. It can lift families out of poverty, send missionaries across the globe, fund orphanages, plant churches, and bring clean water to villages that have never had it. It can sponsor single moms, feed the hungry, and create businesses that give people dignity and purpose.

Throughout history, there's been a strange tension between faith and finances. Some early church movements leaned toward asceticism, equating holiness with poverty. But Scripture paints a broader picture. God blessed Abraham, Joseph, David, and others not so that they could hoard wealth—but so that they could be a blessing. As Deuteronomy 8:18 reminds us, *"It is He who gives you the ability to produce wealth."*

So let's stop apologizing for a blessed, prosperous life, and start stewarding it well. Money doesn't make you holy—but it can help you make a holy impact. When your heart is right, money isn't the root of evil—it's the seed of possibility.

There are many scriptures in the Bible where God expresses His desire to bless His people. While an exact count is difficult, various sources list dozens of Bible verses that highlight God's blessings. Here are just a few.

- Deuteronomy 8:18 – "But remember the LORD your God, for it is he who gives you the ability to produce wealth."
- Genesis 12:2-3 – "I will bless you and make your name great, and you shall be a blessing."

- Deuteronomy 28:2 – "All these blessings shall come upon you and overtake you, if you obey the Lord your God."
- Psalm 115:12 – "The Lord has been mindful of us; He will bless us."
- Malachi 3:10 – "Bring the whole tithe into the storehouse... and see if I will not throw open the floodgates of heaven and pour out so much blessing."

What is Wealth?

Many people equate wealth with money, but Kris Vallotton, in his book *Poverty, Riches, and Wealth*, teaches that true wealth is abundance in every area of life—spiritual, relational, and financial. He challenges the mindset that poverty is spiritual and instead encourages believers to embrace God's provision.

Myles Munroe also taught that wealth is not just financial prosperity but the ability to maximize your potential and impact the world.

True Success: The Story of John D. Rockefeller

Few individuals have shaped the world of business and philanthropy as profoundly as John D. Rockefeller. He was one of the wealthiest men in history, yet his legacy wasn't just about money—it was about faith, generosity, and purpose.

Rockefeller built Standard Oil, transforming the oil industry and amassing unprecedented wealth. But despite his financial success, he understood that money alone wasn't the measure of a life well-lived. He believed that God had entrusted him with wealth, and it was his responsibility to use it wisely.

Rockefeller gave away more than half a billion dollars in his lifetime, funding churches, hospitals, education, and medical research. He established the University of Chicago, supported missionary work, and helped eradicate diseases through his philanthropic efforts.

His guiding principle was simple:

"I believe the power to make money is a gift from God...to be developed and used to the best of our ability for the good of mankind."

Rockefeller's life teaches us that true success is not just about accumulating wealth—it's about using it for God's glory. He didn't let money control him; instead, he used it to serve others.

Lessons from Rockefeller's Life:

- Success is stewardship—wealth is a tool, not a goal.
- Generosity multiplies blessings—giving leads to lasting impact.
- Faith and business can coexist—you can honor God while excelling in your career.

Rockefeller's story is a powerful reminder that true success is found in faith, generosity, and purpose.

Scriptures on Success and Wealth:

Success Through God's Help and Guidance:

- Joshua 1:8 – "Keep this Book of the Law always on your lips; meditate on it day and night, so that you may be careful to do everything written in it. Then you will be prosperous and successful."

- Proverbs 16:3 – "Commit to the LORD whatever you do, and he will establish your plans."
- Psalms 1:1-3 – "Blessed is the one who does not walk in step with the wicked . . . but whose delight is in the law of the LORD . . . whatever they do prospers."

Wealth as a Blessing and Responsibility

- Deuteronomy 8:18 – "But remember the LORD your God, for it is he who gives you the ability to produce wealth."
- Proverbs 10:22 – "The blessing of the LORD brings wealth, without painful toil for it."
- 1 Timothy 6:17 – "Command those who are rich in this present world not to be arrogant nor to put their hope in wealth, which is so uncertain, but to put their hope in God."

Balancing Wealth and Faith:

- Matthew 6:24 – "No one can serve two masters. Either you will hate the one and love the other, or you will be devoted to the one and despise the other."
- Luke 16:10-11 – "Whoever can be trusted with very little can also be trusted with much."
- Matthew 16:26 – "What good will it be for someone to gain the whole world, yet forfeit their soul?"

Balancing Success and Family:

One of the greatest challenges in pursuing success is maintaining balance. Many people sacrifice relationships for ambition, only to realize later that true success includes strong family connections.

Zig Ziglar emphasized that success without family is empty:

"Many people who have achieved financial success have lost their families in the process. True success is having both."

Myles Munroe also warned against neglecting relationships for career goals, teaching that family is the foundation of lasting success.

Examples of Balanced Success:

1. Tim Tebow – Athlete, Author, and Philanthropist.

Tim Tebow rose to fame as a Heisman-winning quarterback, but his success wasn't just about sports; it was about faith and impact. Despite facing criticism and setbacks in his professional career, Tebow remained steadfast in his beliefs, using his platform to serve others.

He founded the Tim Tebow Foundation, which supports children with disabilities, provides medical care, and fights human trafficking. His life demonstrates that true success isn't just about personal achievement—it's about using your gifts to glorify God and help others.

2. Alan Barnhart – Business Leader with a Kingdom Mindset:

Alan Barnhart, the CEO of Barnhart Crane & Rigging, built a highly successful company in the heavy lifting industry. However, from the beginning, he viewed wealth as a responsibility, not a personal reward.

Despite leading a multimillion-dollar business, Barnhart and his family chose to live modestly, capping their personal income at a middle-class level. Instead of accumulating wealth for themselves, they gave away the majority of their profits to fund missions, ministries, and charitable causes.

Barnhart's philosophy was simple:

"God owns the business, and we are just stewards of His resources."

His story proves that success isn't just about financial gain—it's about using wealth to serve God and others.

3. John Maxwell – Leadership Expert and Pastor

John Maxwell is one of the most influential leadership speakers in the world, but his foundation is faith. Before becoming a best-selling author, he was a pastor, and he continues to integrate biblical principles into his teachings.

Maxwell has trained millions of leaders, yet he remains deeply committed to his family and ministry. His success shows that true leadership is about serving others, not just personal ambition.

The Common Thread:

Each of these individuals proves that success is not just about wealth or fame—it's about faith, family, and service. They remind us that true success is measured by impact, integrity, and obedience to God's calling.

Keys to True Success:

1. Define Your Purpose – Success is not just about money; it's about fulfilling your calling.
2. Prioritize Relationships – Success without family is failure.
3. Manage Wealth Wisely – Money is a tool, not the goal.

4. Stay Grounded in Faith – God's principles lead to lasting success.

Your Path to True Success

Success is not just about what you achieve—it's about who you become. If you want true success, pursue purpose, balance, and impact.

Small Group Lesson Chapter 15
True Success

Main Scripture:

"But remember the LORD your God, for it is he who gives you the ability to produce wealth."
—Deuteronomy 8:18

Big Idea:

True success isn't measured by money, status, or comparison—it's found in fulfilling your God-given purpose, stewarding resources wisely, and living a life that glorifies God and serves others.

Opening Discussion:

Icebreaker:
What did you want to be when you grew up? Would that have made you feel "successful"?

Key Points to Explore:

1. Success is About Purpose, Not Possessions
   - Dr. Myles Munroe: *"Success is the fulfillment of purpose."*
   - True success means becoming who God created you to be—not competing with others.
2. Success is Serving Others
   - Zig Ziglar: *"You can have everything in life you want if you help enough other people get what they want."*

- Real success uplifts others; it's rooted in generosity and humility.
3. Money is Not Evil—But It's a Tool
    - The love of money, not money itself, is the root of all evil (1 Timothy 6:10).
    - God gives us the ability to produce wealth—so we can bless others, fund the mission, and impact the world.

Group Questions (10-15 minutes):

1. How do you currently define success? Has that changed over time?
2. Are you chasing the world's version of success or God's calling for your life?
3. How can you use your time, talent, and resources to serve others more intentionally?
4. What does "success with balance" look like for you—in your family, career, and faith?

Scriptures for Reflection:

- Joshua 1:8 – Success through obedience
- Proverbs 10:22 – Wealth without sorrow
- Matthew 16:26 – Soul over success
- 1 Timothy 6:17 – Hope in God, not riches

Next Steps / Challenge (5 minutes):

- This Week's Challenge: Identify *one way* to realign your pursuit of success with your God-given purpose. It could be spending time with your family, helping someone else grow, or sowing into a ministry.
- Prayer Focus: Ask God to redefine your view of success and help you steward your gifts and influence for His glory.

CHAPTER 16

KNOWING GOD!

"You make known to me the path of life; in your presence there is fullness of joy; at your right hand are pleasures forevermore."

—Psalm 16:11

Reggie White's Testimony: True Success in Knowing God:

Reggie White, famously known as the "Minister of Defense," was one of the most dominant defensive players in NFL history. However, his legacy extends far beyond football—his unwavering faith in Jesus Christ was the true foundation of his life.

Raised by his grandmother, Reggie witnessed firsthand the love and reality of God through her example. She never pressured him to attend church, but her love and dedication to God deeply influenced him. At just 13 years old, he made the life-changing decision to surrender his heart to Christ, feeling a strong calling to ministry. By the time he was 17, he had already been ordained as a minister, dedicating his life to spreading the Gospel while pursuing his dream of playing professional football.

Reggie believed his success in football was more than personal achievement—it was an opportunity to share his faith. He often spoke about his belief that God had given him the platform of professional sports to boldly proclaim Jesus. His words reflected his conviction: *"I always believed, since I was a kid, that God was going to allow me to play professional football to use it as a platform to proclaim and to live out the name of Jesus, and that is the most exciting part about my life."*

He Aligned His Life With God's Purpose:

Throughout his career, Reggie remained outspoken about his faith, using his influence to transform lives. He dedicated himself to helping struggling communities by creating job opportunities, renovating homes, and preaching truth and sacrifice. His life was a testament to living out one's faith through action, demonstrating that true success isn't measured by trophies or fame, but by a heart surrendered to God.

True Success Comes From Knowing God – You Need Jesus

Reggie's story serves as a powerful reminder that fulfillment cannot be found in wealth or status—it comes from a deep, personal relationship with God. Many people chase worldly success only to find emptiness, but Reggie knew that true victory is found in surrendering to Christ. His journey was marked by bold faith, unwavering determination, and a commitment to serving others through the love of Jesus.

The Friendship of God: A Relationship, Not Religion

Knowing God is more than following rules or attending church—it's about walking with Him daily, experiencing His love, guidance, and presence. He is not a distant deity but a personal, relational God who desires friendship with His people. Throughout Scripture, we see individuals who didn't just believe in God—they knew Him intimately and walked with Him in deep relationship.

- Moses: A Friend Who Spoke Face to Face
  Moses didn't just receive commandments—he spoke with God directly. Exodus 33:11 says, *"The Lord would speak to Moses face to face, as one speaks to a friend."* His relationship with God was built on trust, obedience, and deep communion.
- David: A Heart After God
  David's life was marked by worship, honesty, and dependence on God. Through victories and failures, he continually sought God's presence. His psalms reveal a man who poured out his heart to God, showing that friendship with Him includes both joy and struggle.
- Abraham: Called a Friend of God
  Abraham's faith was so strong that God called him His friend (James 2:23). He trusted God's promises, even when they seemed impossible, proving that friendship with God is built on faith and surrender.
- Paul: A Life Transformed by Relationship
  Paul went from persecuting Christians to dedicating his life to Christ. His letters reveal a man who walked closely

with God, relying on His strength and wisdom in every challenge.
- Mary Magdalene: A Devoted Follower
Mary Magdalene experienced Jesus' love and redemption firsthand. She wasn't just a believer; she was a devoted friend, present at His crucifixion and the first to witness His resurrection.

When we walk closely with God, life is fuller, richer, and more purposeful. He is not an empty religion but a living, loving Father who wants to guide, strengthen, and walk with us through every season.

My Friendship with God:

Through the years, both in business and ministry, my greatest moments have always been when I was close to the Lord. He is not just my guide—He is my closest friend. Though He is holy and worthy of all reverence, His presence is deeply personal, shaping my every step.

His whispers throughout the day change everything—bringing wisdom, direction, and peace when I need it most. There are times when I open the Bible, feel His presence, and weep at the weight of His love. His wisdom has opened doors I never could, His counsel has shaped lives, and His protection through my travels across continents is undeniable.

Life without Him would be empty, lacking purpose and fulfillment. Even the greatest success would feel hollow without Him at the center. Jesus said in John 10:10 (NIV): *"The thief comes only to steal and kill and destroy; I have come that they may have life, and have it to the full."*

Knowing Him is life itself—and walking with Him brings fullness beyond what the world can offer.

I have tried life without and with Jesus. His love, forgiveness, and companionship have made life worth living. Billy Graham famously said, "I have never known a man who received Christ and ever regretted it."

A Prayer for Salvation

If you're ready to begin a life of true success—the kind that starts with knowing Jesus—then this moment is for you. You don't have to have it all together. Just come as you are, and let Him do the rest. Pray this prayer from your heart:

Salvation Prayer:

> *"Lord Jesus, I come to You just as I am—a sinner in need of Your grace. I believe You died on the cross for my sins and rose again so that I could have eternal life. Today, I surrender my life to You. Be my Lord and Savior. Fill me with Your Holy Spirit and lead me in Your truth. Thank You for loving me and saving me. In Jesus' name, Amen."*

If you just prayed that prayer and meant it with all your heart, welcome to the family of God! You've been born again, and your new life in Christ has begun. The Bible promises He will never leave you or forsake you.

To grow in your new faith, here are a few simple next steps:

- Get a Bible and start reading the book of John—it's a great place to begin understanding who Jesus is.
- Find a church where Jesus is preached and the Bible is taught.
- Join a small group or Bible study—it's a great way to build relationships and grow stronger in your walk with God.

I'm praying for you as you begin this exciting journey. May God lead you, strengthen you, and help you fulfill the dreams He's placed inside your heart.

To help you get started, there are free resources available on my personal website. You don't have to walk this road alone—we're here to walk with you.

My prayer is that you would know Him and turn your God-given dreams into reality!

www.Bob-Pittman.com

Small Group Lesson: Chapter 16 – Knowing God!

Key Scripture:

"You make known to me the path of life; in your presence there is fullness of joy; at your right hand are pleasures forevermore."
—Psalm 16:11

Main Theme:

True success isn't defined by fame, wealth, or achievements—it's found in a real, growing relationship with God. Knowing Him personally transforms your life, gives purpose to your path, and fills your heart with lasting joy.

Icebreaker Question:

What's one achievement or life moment that made you feel proud—but still left you feeling like something was missing?

Testimony Highlight: Reggie White – The Minister of Defense

Reggie White achieved NFL greatness, but he always pointed to a deeper purpose—his relationship with Jesus Christ. He used his platform not to promote himself but to glorify God and serve others. His story reminds us that success without God is hollow, but a life with God is full—even when things aren't perfect.

Discussion Questions:

1. What does it mean to truly "know God" rather than just know about Him?
2. Reggie White believed his football career was a platform to share Jesus. What platform do you have—your job, school, family—that God can use?
3. Look at the examples from Scripture (Moses, David, Mary Magdalene, Paul, Abraham). Which one resonates with you the most, and why?
4. Have you ever had a season where you drifted from your friendship with God? What helped you return?

Application Challenge:

This week, set aside 20 minutes each day to spend quiet time with God. Whether it's reading Scripture, journaling, or praying, commit to nurturing your friendship with Him intentionally.

Ask yourself:

- Am I pursuing God or just going through the motions?
- How can I grow in closeness with Him this month?

Closing Reflection & Prayer Opportunity:

If someone in the group is ready to begin a relationship with Jesus, invite them to pray the salvation prayer at the end of the chapter. Offer encouragement, and plan how the group can support them in their next steps.

Memory Verse:

"The thief comes only to steal and kill and destroy; I have come that they may have life, and have it to the full."

—John 10:10 (NIV)

TOOLS FOR SUCCESS

Healing from Business or Ministry Failures: A Reflective Worksheet

Purpose: This worksheet is designed to help you process the emotional and practical aspects of failure, heal from setbacks, and rebuild confidence to move forward.

Step 1: Identifying What You Are Feeling

Failure can bring a mix of emotions. Take a moment to reflect.

Circle or write down emotions that resonate with you:

- Frustration
- Shame
- Disappointment
- Fear
- Grief
- Hopelessness
- Anger
- Loss of identity
- Other: _____

Reflect:

- What triggered these feelings?
- How do they manifest in your daily life?

Step 2: Dealing with Pain & Wounds

Failure leaves emotional wounds that need intentional healing.

Reflection Questions:

1. What specific event or decision caused this failure?
2. What narratives or negative thoughts have developed because of this?
3. Who or what am I blaming?
4. What would I say to a friend going through the same situation?

Healing Practices:

- Journal about what happened and what you've learned.
- Release blame—whether toward yourself or others.
- Find scriptures or affirmations that speak to your worth.
- Pray or meditate on acceptance and renewal.

Step 3: Getting Healthy Again

Failure can drain you emotionally, physically, and spiritually. Reset and nurture yourself intentionally.

Checklist for Emotional, Physical & Spiritual Health:

- ✓ Prioritize rest and self-care.
- ✓ Surround yourself with life-giving relationships.
- ✓ Engage in a hobby or creative outlet.
- ✓ Exercise or take time outdoors.
- ✓ Deepen your spiritual practices (prayer, worship, fasting).
- ✓ Seek counsel (mentor, pastor, counselor).
- ✓ Set new goals without fear of repeating mistakes.

Write one action you will take this week:

Step 4: Rebuilding Confidence & Moving Forward

You are not defined by failure. Confidence is built through action and perspective shifts.

Reframing Your Story:

- Instead of: "I failed." → **Say:** "I learned a valuable lesson."
- Instead of: "I lost everything." → **Say:** "This is a chance to rebuild stronger."
- Instead of: "I will never succeed." → **Say:** "Success is built on resilience."

Write a Declaration of Confidence:

"I am _____ (worthy/capable/strong). I choose to _____ (rise, rebuild, trust God). This failure will not define me—my future is full of hope."

Step 5: Planning Your Path Forward

Failures teach us what doesn't work—but they also guide us toward new strategies.

Create an action list of steps it will take to rebuild.
- Action List: (Who do I need to meet with, what plans do I need to write, what skill do I need to develop?)
  - o
  - o
  - o
  - o

Reflection Questions:

1. What lessons can I take from this failure?
2. What adjustments will I make moving forward?
3. What areas of growth do I need to focus on?
4. What dream, goal, or vision will I pursue next?
5. What does my **new** plan look like? (Write actionable steps.)
   -
   -
   -
   -
   -

Closing Prayer or Reflection:

Surrender past failures, embrace grace, and commit to the next step. Write a short prayer, affirmation, or scripture that speaks to renewal.

VISION TO REALITY: A DREAM PLANNING WORKSHEET

Purpose: This worksheet will help you define your dream, break it into logical steps, and create a strategy to bring it to life. Whether it's a business, ministry, creative project, or personal goal, structured planning transforms ideas into action.

Step 1: Clarifying Your Dream

Take a moment to articulate your vision.

What is your dream?
Why does this dream matter to you?
Who will it impact? (Yourself, family, community, customers, etc.)
What will success look like?

Step 2: Defining Scope and Goals

Every big dream needs clear objectives and realistic expectations.

Scope:

- Is this a short-term or long-term goal?
- Does this dream require financial investment?
- What knowledge or skills will you need to develop?

SMART Goals (Specific, Measurable, Achievable, Relevant, Time-bound):

1. **Specific:** What EXACTLY needs to be accomplished?
2. **Measurable:** How will you track progress?
3. **Achievable:** Is this realistic with the resources available?
4. **Relevant:** Does this align with your core values and purpose?
5. **Time-bound:** What is your deadline for key milestones?

Write down at least one SMART goal for your dream:

Step 3: Identifying Challenges & Resources

Before moving forward, anticipate obstacles and gather support.

Potential Roadblocks:

- Financial limitations
- Lack of time or expertise
- Fear or self-doubt
- Unclear direction
- Other: _____

Resources & Support:

- Mentors or advisors
- Books, courses, or research materials
- Financial planning (budget, funding)
- Network or community connections
- Personal strengths (skills, experience, faith)

What are three specific actions you can take to overcome challenges?

1.
2.
3.

Step 4: Structuring Your Plan

Break your dream into manageable steps.

Short-Term Steps (Next 3-6 months):

1.
2.
3.

Mid-Term Steps (6-12 months):

1.
2.
3.

Long-Term Steps (Beyond 1 year):

1.
2.
3.

Step 5: Building Momentum & Accountability

Success is built through consistency and reflection.

Accountability Plan:

- How will you stay motivated? (Daily reflection, prayer, affirmations, etc.)
- Who can help keep you accountable? (Mentors, friends, business partners)
- What will you do when faced with setbacks? (Pivot, learn, adjust)

Write a commitment statement to your dream: *"I commit to pursuing _____ with intention and perseverance. I will take the necessary steps, seek guidance, and remain faithful to the process."*

Final Reflection & Prayer

Write a short prayer, affirmation, or scripture that encourages your journey forward.

TIME MANAGEMENT DAILY PLANNER

Date: _____

Day: _____

☐ Schedule: Hour-by-Hour Planning

Time	Task / Appointment
6:00 AM	_____
7:00 AM	_____
8:00 AM	_____
9:00 AM	_____
10:00 AM	_____
11:00 AM	_____
12:00 PM	_____
1:00 PM	_____
2:00 PM	_____
3:00 PM	_____
4:00 PM	_____
5:00 PM	_____
6:00 PM	_____
7:00 PM	_____
8:00 PM	_____
9:00 PM	_____

☐ Top Priorities (List up to four key items for the day)

1. _____

2. _____

3. _____

4. _____

☐ To-Do List (Assign priority level: 1 = High, 2 = Medium, 3 = Low)

Task	Priority (1–4)	Done (✓)
_____	_____	_____
_____	_____	_____
_____	_____	_____
_____	_____	_____
_____	_____	_____
_____	_____	_____

☐ Notes & Reminders

_____
_____
_____
_____

☐ End-of-Day Review
- What was accomplished today?
  _____
- What needs follow-up tomorrow?
  _____
- Lessons learned or reflections:
  _____

Daily Walk with God Devotional:

☐ Daily Devotional Worksheet

Date: _____ Day: _____

☐ Scripture Reading
Today's Bible Passage: _____

Key Verse or Insight:
_____
_____
_____

☐ What Did God Speak to Me Today?
Take a moment to reflect on what you felt the Lord was showing you through His Word, prayer, or life circumstances.
_____
_____
_____
_____
_____

☐ Prayer Requests
Write down people, situations, or areas of life that need prayer.

1.

2.

3.

4.

☐ Spiritual Goals for Today
Set a focus or action step to live out your faith today.

☐ Praise & Thanksgiving
List any answered prayers or blessings you're grateful for.

☐ Personal Reflections or Journal Notes
Use this space for anything else on your heart—dreams, challenges, insights, or encouragement.

BOB PITTMAN and his wife, Char, serve as Senior Pastors of World Harvest Church in Rice Lake, Wisconsin. Before stepping into full-time ministry, Bob enjoyed a successful career as an executive in the software industry. With a passion for both business and ministry, Bob has led companies, preached internationally, taught the Bible, and spoken at seminars. He is especially known for ministering the love and power of Jesus through the gifts of the Holy Spirit. Together, Bob and Char are devoted to mentoring and equipping leaders to fulfill their God-given calling.

www.ingramcontent.com/pod-product-compliance
Lightning Source LLC
Chambersburg PA
CBHW032105090426
42743CB00007B/235